NOTE TO SELF

NOTE TO SELF

An Original Book of Inspirational Aphorisms

VINCENT JOHN LECCE

Vincent John Lecce

1

Note to Self:
An Original Book of Inspirational Aphorisms
by Vincent John Lecce

*I must think – and in between that, I must write.
To think and write, to myself and for you, to share
with those who read and think, this is a handbook: a
book for life:
a life that is much more than our own.*

1. Write at least once every day and date it. If not write, then think... about the lessons I've learned... about the way I will pave.
2. Enthuse yourself to live: how could someone

possibly do that? A start: think happily to yourself. This can mean thinking about the paradise outside of your home, inside of your home; your freedom to breathe, live, and act in anyway every day; your access to fresh water, time, and space; your world to move and think and pursue. Happy are the thoughts that come from all this and more, up to your creativity, ingenuity, and imagination.

3. You are the ruler of your consequences; own up to the responsibility of your actions.
4. Keep going even when you appear down and out. You can, and will, still *try*, no matter how little effort is made, no matter how little or large the task. You will keep moving on – it's the nature of our world. But if you *do* try *not* to move on, you could end up suffering the consequences: swimming against the current, the opposite way, the *wrong way* When you *do*, when you *try*, you must **let go** to face no harsh consequences.
5. Keep your head on – **strong** – and protect yourself from bad behaviour, negative

words, and negative thinking. Eliminate such thoughts, words, and behaviour with thinking, "*Remove all evil behaviour, all my evil words, all my evil thoughts. Replace them with **goodness** in deeds, words, and thought.*" This will rid you of delusion, greed, fear, and the chaos of evil. *Remove all evil with **thought** and **action**.*

6. Stick by your friends and keep your word to them. Protect them and be by their side in the face of danger, of their dangers, of their own fears. Remember you are nothing but friends, family, neighbours, or strangers to the people around you, as acquaintances are neighbours, friends like family. Likewise, you will stand by, keep your word, and protect *your family* from disconnect, evil, and harm. Be good in your relations and do not – *ever* – treat evil with another form of evil.

7. Remove all inclination toward selfish desire – including pursuing a girl, food, material goods – so you can maintain a healthy and stable diet, consisting of good food, healthy relations, and wholesome reads. Avoid excess

at all extents. Cultivate **self-restraint** and selectivity, one of many virtues to live up to... all within time.

8. Deepen your values and widen your perspective with planning and research. *We have access to the internet at almost all times* – your mind at ***all*** times.
9. Keep up the good work, great deeds, and public conversation. You are meant to be a friendly, social being, so ***act like it***. Care and be one with both what and who is around you.
10. Loosen up from stress with the art of balance in daily living. Compassion, love, and celebrating the joy of others are right at your doorstep, so, invite them in, and invite them to stay. What else for balance than hard work, good people, and an evening to relax?
11. Do what you have set out to do – *after contemplation* – every time. As you begin, *do not look too far back*.
12. Power through laziness, boredom, sleepiness, and other physical and mental fetters.

Be a *man*... although there must be some **caution here**: To be a man, you must *show* your manliness in the face of adversity – '*being a man*' means pushing through the pains of mental, physical, and emotional suffering, not pushing through with masculinity. Execute endurance, strength, and courage; act courageously even if you are indifferent to any sexual delineation, even if you do not know your own sexual identity. If you have yet to define who you are, you still have the chance to uncover what your identity means for you and the courage you show it in its performance.

13. Keep calm, as equanimity is your center. *Equanimity?* – composure in all forms all 'round.
14. Head strong, heart open, to and for kindness, to and for gentleness, and to and for generosity. However, maintaining a strong mind means to defend your heart against inevitable negati-vities. Be as smart as is required to defend your heart.
15. Build yourself up to be the person you choose

to be. Guidance from research, friends, family, and travel will help, but never forget your own guidance, your own *self*.

16. Distinguish the qualities of a good person from a bad, a sly, an indecent, a *mad* Discern cautiously or befriend the bad over the good. *Never classify someone as a friend until they reveal their true character in moments of unsolicited disclosure.* The difference should be evident at most times whether one is true or foggy, cunning, or base.

17. Maintain peace, composure, and a mix of friendliness in all circumstance. Remember to speak openly to those who you know well; do not be pompous or boastful; speak the truth and watch your words before you say them to those who you do not yet know. Limit your words to make them few; make words *meaningful – relevant – No one likes talk without substance.* To create and maintain substance, think before you speak within the context of conversation. You will see people have more to say than you think.

18. Keep friends who come to *you* to hang out knowing that they are good people. Initiate

when the time is opportune for you both. Time is opportune when you both work together and finish work together, when you go to school, eat lunch and grab a drink together when you are both free and available. However, do *not*place much time on going out to spend time together; make your time limited, and, therefore, meaningful.*Less is more*, even when it comes to friendship or relationships.

19. Think of everything you can do to plan your good deeds, especially when it comes down to keeping your word to a friend. *Keep your words true!* – (I cannot write or say this enough).

20. Socialize, but never to turn the situation over to your favour. At times, you must let conversation happen to you, from others, and not instigate or interrupt conversation. At other times, the people who are around you are simply not in the mood, not the type of person to want to talk, are not interested to converse as openly and as freely as you do. Taking no response back to your spoken or written words personally is a crime to

yourself alone. Do not throw yourself in bars. Be free enough to let the silence speak for itself.

21. "*Little by little, you can go far.*" With the right methods, a smart approach, some steps by small steps, a long distance can amount to a great end. Without small steps, you may suffer by the hands of pressure, over-ambitiousness, over-extension and overexertion. Burnout is the *enemy*; gradual effort is your *friend*.

22. Why do you go towards alcohol to stay strong? Why do you overcompensate for your pain? Why wouldn't you endure through it instead? What *ideas* or *people* are stopping you from sobriety? What would it take to show yourself you can be *clean*? Anyone can pass through their situations with some change and little bravery, although the road is bumpy, not straight. Yet it is time to step up and show yourself *your truer self*, what you really want to be.... (to an old friend of mine).

23. *From Confucius*: Always notify your guardians where you are going and how long

you will be there, staying put on travel, especially abroad. Short distances, as well, should be known to them; you never know what advice or reminders they could hand out to you in the last minute of your departure. Even if none comes out at all, accept the advice you give to yourself while travelling close to home or abroad, to keep your word, to manage your time, to travel smart, and with good company.

24. *Aim to love the whole world.* I am not kidding, the **whole**

25. Studiousness develops the mind and its thoughts while keeping them in check. Discern what to study – what is good for you – and what not to study – what is unwholesome or unnece-ssary. The thoughts you think determine the live you lead... which also depends on what thoughts and ideas you feed.

26. Be *wary* of the company you keep, and, again, keep its time to a minimum. Precious moments are those that are *rare*; keep good friendships as rare as they can be.

27. Cherish what you've got – it could have all been gone by now.
28. Keep productive by fine-tuning your independence. **Independence** means being free to act, speak, and think on your own; to consider your own terms to your own conditions; to work your load while figuring out your moves without asking another's permission; to keep your worries and doubts to yourself unless asked to disclose; to settle enduring times by yourself. You alone are the one whose affairs you will settle. You go about affairs alone to work on your own terms, to persist with effort, to maintain a good stance on your lot of responsibilities, not impose your manageable load onto another. So, keep at it in your head that you must strive *now* to manage your duties. You only have all the time left in the world... and time is catching up to you. Latch onto your time, then: take on the responsibility to be independent even around other people and especially among the company you keep all alone. As cliché as it may sound, one is

never lonely while in good company – *even among oneself.*

29. All things must pass away – ephemerality is everywhere and in everything. Things may become more joyful once all suffering has come to its end, as all suffering will pass away. Therefore, *continue*, and you will live in the joy that you may seek.

30. Communicate softly – soft enough that no ego or self can be heard or seen. *Silence your ego and the world can be heard through another.*

31. Compassion starts with others in mind and ends with others felt in heart. An accomplishment is to finally place your mind upon their heart, to hear its beating, to stare at its lot, to recognize exactly what they've had, and what exactly what they've now got.

32. Rhyme without reason alone when it is sought.

33. Freedom is a matter of everyone's aim, but to choose freedom is to actively *limit* what you've got. *Limit what you've **for** freedom? You must be nuts.* Freedom is a matter of *choice* **and** of *limit*. To choose what you've got and

what you've got to give wisely, structure freedom within bounds and borders. This is the security of freedom: to liberate yourself from unbound desire. *Limit yourself, then set yourself free.*

34. Thoughts when helping others: Give as much as you can, and twice the amount of that; offer all the truth you can give out, all the attention you can pay; be there when someone's in need; keep helpful eyes open to a helpful view in sight. Cultivate patience to seek and complete work together with whom you help; never drift away half-complete when you know more can be done; keep loyal to your duties – to be there when in one's need; help yourself first, or, at best, others at the same time. These thoughts may help you, too.

35. When in doubt, research, study, observe your surroundings, and question: *"What am I doing?"*, *"What else could be done?"* Answer, immediately, and think: *"I am doing my job – to serve others and serve myself; to be free; to be happy with good mind and good choice. What to be done is to fulfill my role, to play my part,*

and work towards understanding. With balance of heart and mind, work towards compassion." Keep your mind agile, options open, to make your final call. Serve yourself, once and for all.

36. Duty. Wisdom. Love. Courage. These and all the other virtues lack the attention they deserve in our day in age and generation. Ignite their according actions instead. Take on their challenges to enlighten those who have turned, mentally and physically, dull and wavy. Remove all fetters towards happiness – it is you who is in control of your own. Yours is through courage, not pleasures or other feeble desires. Learn what base living means through *observation* and *thought*, **not** by its experience. *If you cannot help it, keep the lessons you live through till the end.*

37. Make what you take out of living and attempt to make it great. What is *living*? Your situation, or the action in your life, the people, your place, your circumstance. Encourage others just as much as you do for yourself to live your life happily, doing what you rightly do to make it so. *Never harm or*

injure yourself or another; freedom means freedom for others, too. (This means not to disrespect your body, mind, or their unity [when it arrives] as well).

38. Climb up over those walls you have built up around your heart; your mind is there to remove, or *reconstruct*, its foundation.
39. Inspire to build up a life with human effort and a steady drive. Keep forward as you steer and pick up those who could be, should be, taken for the ride. Do *not*, however, when you come about it, miss their final stop.
40. Enter your mind with joy as much as with your suffering. With composure as your cure, love yourself as you have love for those close to you. Nurture the good through the bad and witness the goodness grow.
41. Remove the stone within your shoe; eliminate complaint. Be mindful of your pains and throbs. Know you are better than those who complain, but better are those who, themselves, they restrain. While the mind is unlimited, suffering seems so, too. Therefore, mind your suffering just as you mind your mind. All is time, ebb and flow, seam-

lessly to our end. *You must endure until you determine what's your final end.*

42. If ever infected by laziness, you have either kept bad company, bad habit, or not strengthened your will. So, *necessarily*, strengthen your will, keep good company, and be mindful of the habits that you keep. Another habit may grow out of you – those habits of will and good action. *What is a good act?* Study and live in **virtues** well, then see.

43. Stay optimistic about the limits you set on your freedom. "*Less is more*," speaks truth (I'll say it again if I have to). With more time to do moderate activity, you grow closer to mastery – to perfect your crafts and your activities. *Remain optimistic as you work towards the greatness of your craft!* You have whatever you need both inside and around you.

44. The meaning of your life is found in thought, in action, in word, and in choice. Be wary of each and attempt *greatness...* – however, greatness does not mean self-importance. Aim to be satisfied by your words, strengthened by your deeds, enlightened by your thoughts, and inspired by your choices.

Greatness means to do what you have sought out to do… and more.

45. Act. Speak. Perform – what you know: your obligations. Each duty will amount to their own treasure, yet you pursue them for other reasons – you aim to do them for their own sake, for their own completion, by their own virtue, in their own respect. *Perform, and then step back; see the rewards all come straight back* – to you and for those you love.

46. Never depreciate your value. You are one of the billions of people living in this world. Be happy you are **alive**. You made it and you can go farther. *Move on, further, toward your worth, happiness, and future.*

47. Family first, friends who are like family, then acquaintances, and people in general. You are equal to the workings of your family – those who are immediate and those closest to you. Family will influence you in ways you cannot see at first glance, so you must choose who you spend time with **wisely**. Prioritize the people who you are worthy of your time and you will turn all right right on ahead.

48. *Take only what is given and do not ask for more* – a challenge – – yes, it is – but one for the sake to accept what you're given without compliant or greed. It's all you've got for now, so make the very most of it all. *Count your blessings, as they say. Figure who and how much you have already along your way.*
49. **Lead for yourself**, not the others around you, *unless given a proper role to do so.*
50. Reading, learning, and knowing these passages and reminders, people may take advantage of your goodness. Hold yourself up high – choose what to take on and what not to consider. Favours at work? – sure. Favours for strangers? – be wary. Errands for friends or strangers? – unacceptable. Favours for friends? – always. Differentiate errands from favours, differentiate the close from the far.
51. Spend time with those you care about without being overbearing. Balance time between friends, work, personal care, and your hobbies and activities. Friends, however, deserve time, just as work, personal care, and activity. While spending your time, use it up

wisely. Be smart through **discernment**: what is worthy of your time. Plan your day ahead, and balance your damn precious time.

52. Direct yourself whenever you get the chance or have the mind to do so – *you always have the mind to do so*. Whenever you feel the need to control anything, always choose to control *yourself*. Guard against directing others or asking any favours.

53. Choose your endeavour(s) while you are given the chance. Read, write, work, create, and attend to family and friends. Be open to chance encounters. Be mindful about your attention to these endeavours and they will serve you well, *just as well* as you can serve others. *Serve others well as well.*

54. Remember to tie compassion together with detachment. Remain objective in your mind toward the well-being of others as well as your own. *Be compassionate, be objective, and, then, be free.*

55. Make some room for downtime in your schedule, to space yourself out with some space for yourself. Unwind as you eat, unravel your thoughts as you meditate, be

mindful of others throughout the day as you work – your ultimate and final break will come soon: of silence, of peace, of the night.

56. Analyze unclear thoughts. Make thought open to scrutiny to make it clear to you. Then, as you speak, you will be as clear as can be. Openness in speech will save your life with saying what you know as well as the lives of other people who do not know what you'd mean until you'd speak. In an honest word, there is hope. In a clear mind, there are clear intentions and reasons. Know yourself well by the thoughts you clear in time.

57. Eliminate your cravings for the betterment of yourself. Lessen up any burdens you carry by putting in effort to let them go. Gentleness will also be easier with loosening yourself up. Fortitude is easier as you become lighter, *not heavier*. Any other virtue that will come to you will come naturally as you understand the importance of lightening up your load. *Be simple, be human, be free.*

58. Virtue is the way. Embody it well and often – you have every right to master all you know, and all you will soon discover. So, *act*

in virtue of you – of your best intentions and actions.

59. Do not become discouraged by failure, as failure is inevitable in our imperfect world. Never forget, however, to strive to perfect *yourself*, no matter how much failure you undergo in your life. Let the failure fall along with you. Success comes out of trial-and-error; consider *this* 'mistake' trial-and-error. *There are no real mistakes until you determine them as such.*

60. Make peace with sadness, distress, ill-mind, and confusion. Practice being mindful of your happiness, your neutrality, of your negative energies. Learn to compose yourself in neutrality, but be honest in whatever you feel. *Since you are always changing, there is nothing wrong with considering the inconsistencies in yourself.* However (and this is a required counter), slowly attempt to eliminate the contradictions as you now see them, one by one, by one... *by one.*

61. Numbers are not important, people are. Salaries are components of our well-being, **not** **our** **whole** well-being. Self-interest is

necessary, yet interest in others is, too. Make this change in your mind: express the joy of knowing what matters.

62. Don't let your knowledge, goodness, or 'greatness', get to your head. Remind yourself of your own imperfections, like your ignorance, to perfect the balance of a tame mind and wholesome body – a body of knowledge and as a human being. Your goodness differentiates you from others and your goodness aids you better than those who could do something but don't try. The balance of your mind and body comes from acting naturally and freely, not from trying too hard, from worrying about others. *Humble yourself – you are not so grand after all... we all are, naturally, so human.*

63. You're more important than you may know; you're less important than you might think.

64. *Think less of yourself to know more about **you**.*

65. It's both funny and sad how in a world of billions of people we let so few of them either drag us along or bring us down. Move away from the burdens placed on you by others; the weight from another's load is

simply not worth your time. *However*, when in a close relationship with another, *assist them* in their burdens to lighten their load just as you would with your own.

66. Aim to speak the truth. Truth is all that really matters, more than morals, ethics, or any of these passages and reminders. *Aim to speak the truth.* Don't let false speech take the best from you, "even in jest" – a Buddhist principle.

67. Toss aside the past as if it were unnecessary unless you forward reminders of what is relevant to the present moment or you plan ahead. What's past is not worth holding onto unless there are good memories to share or important facts to rise to the surface. The moment here is so animate and alive and present; the past is intangible; there is so much to finish *here*. Be *here*, and not *there*. Realize your presence and know you are **alive**.

68. Be diplomatic and objective in all your affairs. You will find your situation favourable for you and the people around you – with those who you speak to, work with, look

toward for advice, and *live with* – as your diplomatic demeanour holds strong.

69. Expect nothing to happen... or, at most, prepare for *anything* to happen.
70. Independence is necessary, but so is cooperation. Cooperation creates harmony, two ideals to strive for that are away from isolation and *in*solation from other people. *Independence* means growing in knowledge, in your own mind, by your own hands; *interdependence* means to accept that you could not be independent alone.
71. Impress no one, or at best seek not to. Acknowledge your true intentions and admit them to yourself. If you recognize an intention is not in your nature, question where it comes from to expose it, to embrace the intention. If you feel ashamed, guilty, or embarrassed about your true intention, breathe in while saying to yourself, "*I breathe in*"; breathe out while saying to yourself, "*I breathe out*". The practice of composure and quiet patience will lead you to inner peace. This will give you the energy to deal with moments of negative energy. Say to yourself

"I feel ashamed, I feel guilty, I feel embarrassed, yet I am still here, and I am, and will be, okay." By naming true emotions and personal qualities, you will come closer to your own truth and understanding, to become more of what you really are. (I try it now, to embrace my intentions: *Why do I write these passages and reminders? To help myself remember? – Why? – for others to acknowledge the wisdom I think I possess? – to impress others? – to stand out? Am I pretentious? Am I self-seeking? Am I interested in my "self"? Don't I know that the 'self' is not real? – that there is no good reason to seek to be wise? – that we are all impermanent, imperfect, and ever-changing? For what good purpose do I seek other's attention? Lend to yourself your own attention to what troubles you, puzzles you, on events that cause grief and misery. Know that **acknowledgement** is necessary only to aid other people. Help others to think, to inspire them to do more than spend time with technology, and to speak well of others and themselves. Classify your own true needs and intentions and note where to improve them. Encourage, strengthen, and unify people in kindness, friendliness, and*

joy – this you can do to improve, these you can substitute as your true intentions).

72. Strive in your mind to keep it active and push your energy forward for you to **think**. Let go of unnecessary thoughts about what people may say about you to unload any unwanted concerns from your mind. Allow mental energy to flourish in your created art, without allowing it to waste away doing nothing throughout your day. *Do something and*

73. Through research, and good thought, plan and strategize your **priority**: the day to come ahead. Schedule a day to let good thought unfold, keeping time open for action and the unexpected. Planning yourself out will help you to get going, so plan now and get going! *"To be is to do"* – Immanuel Kant.

74. If you know your destination, search up its route. Begin driving, biking, or walking. With each step, in each slight twist and turn, and every weighted pedal forward, you come closer towards your goal. Steer yourself right into its lot. Watch your surroundings and soon settle into your destination –

your destiny. Fated or not, we have come thus far *from our own and others' directions.*

75. Breaks are needed when you are moving faster than the car in front of you. Remember where you are and what you have to do – be mindful, attentive, and *slow down*. Save yourself from crashing – *do not get ahead of yourself.*

76. *"Never let a thought pass by unattended. Complete every thought"* – inspired by an old friend.

77. Be inspired by those you meet and give just as much as you can to inspire others. Reciprocity is the way – it is freedom.

78. Overcome fear, pain, fantasy, lust, delusion, and greed with a proper, well-functioning mind and its according thought. Make peace with your imagination and your unwanted ill-will. Find what you must correct from these defilements in you. With goodness in thought, speech, and action, attempt to embrace all contents of your mind and movement of your body openly. Do not disregard an improper thought, but correct it accordingly. *Correction is the way to a solution.*

79. Everyone has their story. Acknowledge this when you cannot bear another's presence.
80. Why admit defeat now when you have come so far? Why come so far to only admit defeat?
81. Do your work diligently as you abstain from laziness. It is a hindrance that will always hold you back – action as the way forward, inaction as the way back.
82. When you break a rule, or forget to act on a reminder, make up for the lapse in judgment. Bend over backwards for your principles and be true to them, to others, and to you.
83. Avoid temptation, indulgence, and all bodily and mental obstacles. Aim to rid your mind and body of all its defilements to put them to sleep for good – for the *good in you*. List them to put them to rest: laziness, anger, lust, hatred, greed, envy, selfish desire, delusion, maltreatment (of others and of yourself), and ill-will. Name, target, shoot, and lay them to rest. Destruction of the bad for the creation of what is good is the way out of destroying yourself. *Create*

84. Choose health and safety over pride and glory any day. Your rights triumph over your ego. *Your rights are the way to virtue.*
85. Keep your words simple and sentences as clear and direct as you can. There is no need for length in explanation. Your behaviour should be explained only to yourself or when asked by another. Actions speak as a simple explanation to those who observe. *Observe others as you would want them to observe you.*
86. Make way for the changes you will face. Plans change, and so will you. Aim for stability of mind, of character, of heart. Be true to yourself. No matter how much you change, your goodness in virtue can remain the same.
87. Pick each other up from failure when battles grow tough and bonds gather strength. United in solidarity for what's good and what's right is the way true friends will be – inspired *despite* old friends.
88. When headed for the worst, break and turn a 180. In that way, you will change direction to head for better, or even *the best* you now know. Work from the best that you know

and the best will surely come – at least: to you, and at most: to others.

89. Never complain. Others have it so much worse. You have what you have and can even make it better. By your own two hands, using your own two eyes, ears, and one heart, mouth, and mind, speak what's true to make things better than you could ever complain about. Irritation can be handled, complaint can be abstained from, and anger can be tamed. So, *tame, handle, abstain*, and speak with truth and gratitude about your lot and situation.

90. When you want to stop, *continue*. As you reach for a break, reach out towards your **duty** All your actions amount to all you have; make your actions last in their effects. Support yourself and leave something behind for others to follow. However, you must show *yourself* first.

91. Finish what you have started – play it all out. Don't leave, even a mistake – *anything* – to be undone, but '*correct it immediately after the fact*' – paraphrased by the words of Our

Holiness, The Dalai Lama XIV. Finish what you have already begun and never leave anything undone: work, school, or the love of another.

92. Trust your instincts when a feeling of evil is about. Be wary; check your actions, words, thoughts, and emotions... especially deeds. Embrace what keeps you living in fear to loosen up its grip. This is will bring about compassion and understanding for your own suffering and those of others, as well as rid you of fear. *Embrace your fear, but **only** as it comes to you.*

93. Never deny a moment where you can work on your own practice and patience. Cultivate and restore the power of virtue in your character. *There is more than one virtue that you can cultivate.* Begin humbly in respect to your rights and freedoms.

94. Love your neighbour as yourself – *you know this*. Remain objective about it; treat others and yourself no differently – help, support, and be present with people, animals, plants, and insects. We are the same in that we all are living, in that we live.

95. Respect yourself by balancing out (scheduling out) the things that make your life your own. Do you love your family, yet love your personal space? Want time for yourself, yet time with and around others? Make a commitment to get out of the house *and* to stay in your home. Contradiction? – timing and balance unites the two goals.
96. Practice a skill every day, every chance you get, whether it be writing, music, or reading about the world or fictional ones. Learning is a skill, too, so practice *every day*.
97. Mindfully follow your conduct and your business where you are right now. Notice the sounds of your surroundings and name them as they pass by. Practicing calm observance is just one goal to attain.
98. Only share if asked, if you should really notify, or if it will spark belonging and harmony in others and yourself. Never boast when you see that you can. Subtle and plain speech, truth with no vanity: these are some goals to strive towards. Aim for them despite a lack of inhibition; *cultivate inhibition from the unnecessary.*

99. Tranquility and joy, peace and liberation from evils, are your primary aims. Objectivity is the objective, reason and intuition are guides, inspiration from others: all vehicles towards your aims. Riches are available in worthy acts, right speech, and proper thought. These riches are not necessarily for the body, but for the mind – a far worthier realm of human existence.

100. Breathe in and think, but do not when in flow with the present; breathe out in the present and continue the flow with all you know is around you. What is flow? – *the action of movement in harmony with mind and body towards an attainable personal goal.*

101. 'Calm through the storm' can refer to yourself – calm within the troubles of your day, with the mistakes that you've made, with anxieties you have some control over. Open yourself up and the reward will be twofold: calm for self and calm for another. What is better? – both are the same.

102. Let things happen after your planning and careful thought. Prepare for the scene – of your experience, of your life – with focus

and preparation. Make your scene as beautiful as you are with the honesty of your voice and the work of your hands. Rejoice, for you are already ready – ready for your scene.

103. Laugh at yourself and some of the mistakes you make. Correct the great ones *immediately*, while you still have a chance to do so.

104. Home and family are the significant areas of your life. Speak true to them through your words and actions. Act naturally as you do in your consideration for them. Enjoy the time you spend even when settling the most dreadful of situations together. Stay at home while you still can. Form your lasting bonds, again, *while you can.* However, and this is a big however, do so only when they are of sound mind, when they are out for the best for you, when they love and know you and care.

105. Spend time to analyze the parts of your experience part by part, limb from limb: '*Here* is anger, attached to its larger component, hatred, which turns into a disgust in your qualities, that has an aim to destroy yourself.' *Do not destroy yourself.* Instead, tame

your anger as tenderly as you would a child. '*Here* is attention, diverted by mental obstacles – songs in your head, words from a friend, voices from the past. *There* is undivided and penetrating, while *here* is divided and unwholesome. *There* is freedom from delusion – clear and one-pointed direction – *here* is disturbed focus in flux.' *Describe* the mental phenomena in your head. Cleanse your mind with penetrating clarity in the conscious process. Process the happenings in your head and release yourself from worries and dread. Let your mind be your friend. *Inspired by Thich Nhat Hanh.*

106. It is a small world out there. Do not be surprised by how deeply things are connected – objects, people, places, circumstance. Develop and maintain peace with the parts – the parts of our world – to keep calm in the presence of the coincidences of the whole. *It is more coincidence than it is 'meant to be', as coincidence happens naturally.*

107. Rid yourself of irritability. How you do this: replace "*rid yourself of*" with "*make peace with.*" Recognize when it arises and call its

name as it presents itself. Then, talk to your irritability: "*I know you come up every so often, and that is fine by me. Just know that your righteous place is here, in my head, and never out of my mouth. Please respect these boundaries and help spread the peace.*" This can be said to irritability's friends: anger, resentment, and hatred as well.

108. Determine your purpose for true action, your true intention, regardless of how you take the truth. If doing an action out of greed, then call it greedy; if speaking out of spite, then call it out of anger, or of hostility. Your truth will penetrate the roots of your intention to break it down into its parts – its purpose, how it arises, and how it can be replaced. Only make sure to replace the negative intention for a positive. This way you can correct your view into a way more real for your thoughts, purposes, and processes.

109. Never quit – *ever* – not even after any hard failure or hardship. We determine what is hard for ourselves, and we also surprise ourselves on how well we can do what is hard. Difficult situations determine our strength,

yet we *always have enough strength*. Therefore, we can endure our difficulty, whatever it may be now or will be later. *The past doesn't determine the whole future, but the present determines what comes.*

110. You have it in you to do, act, speak, and choose your proper duties. Choose to act and consider all that you can do with what you're given – this is *resourcefulness*. Think, as well, of what you cannot or should not do that may harm yourself or others at large. Drive yourself out of idling – in speech and in mind – and get out there in the world (or at home) to start moving towards your goals. One day, all of what you have in you will be tormented by what you did not do that you *could have done*... so, *start moving*. Time's up, time's now. Get up and at it.

111. Think as long you need before you speak. Words can be more powerful than actions in one's memory. Good deeds strike another cord, one of righteousness, one of no verbal explanation necessary. This is the importance of both word and action. This is the

importance of thoughtfulness in speech and behaviour.

112. *Don't allow your good qualities to get to your head.* Remember what needs to be worked on, your weaknesses. And, for your own sake, remember your past faults. *You're not perfect, but you can try it out for size.*

113. Follow *your* lead, not your mind or anyone else's; your mind is not under your control when it is swayed by anything apart from your true determination. Look to your mind's resources: maybe thought, maybe calculation, maybe to seek or to observe. Break these elements down into simple terms for yourself, for your mind and for its ease to work naturally. For every problem, say to yourself, "*This is a setback I now face. But there is a way out – this will pass. I may not like the solution, but keeping the problem will always be worse. So, what can I do? Reason, be creative, talk, think, act. Choose one or another; be confident in your choice. And the consequences will speak of your choice, so listen to yourself carefully.*" Follow *carefully*.

114. An abundance of freedom will lead to misery and boredom only when no activity is allowed. *No* activity is *not allowed.*
115. Standardize your off-time as a simple habit. You will never be lost in what you could be doing when you always have a back-up plan. Plan small things first to then work on the bigger, uncommon tasks to work on your habits. Productivity is part of your goal. *Be prepared* – inspired by a girl I once well knew....
116. To never change is to forever remain the same – this is clear. We can never ask of ourselves "*never change.*" Our "selves" are made up of ever-changing parts, ones that are never stable for long. What *can* remain stable is our firm, constant resolve: to do our best, to try after we fail, to grow without plateau, to work, act, and do without cessation. In these ways, we *can* forever remain the same. *Practice and see for yourself.*
117. *Appreciate.* All things, big and small, are here for us to be thankful for. All we have is to have and hold, to embrace for a short time. The nature of our universe is that *nothing*

ever lasts for long. What *does* last are our moments together here and now, our good memories, our optimism toward the future; what *doesn't* includes our suffering from the past, in the present, or what's coming in the future. *Nothing ever lasts*. Appreciate this. This is a blessing. *Thank you.*

118. Ask for nothing in return. Do this by seeking simplicity in what you've already got. With want of nothing more and nothing less we achieve serenity and freedom from the incessant want of more. *'Less is more' is a blessing*, having less is no curse. For too many things owned, when they amount to so much, will always end for you turning towards what you don't have, always at reach for what's not truly yours, for the worse. Enjoy the blessing. Avoid the curse. *'Less is more'* first.

119. Finish a page, or a chapter, each time you begin to read or write. See how far you can *really* Allow for outside appearances – other people – to be the only obstacle, one you must face when it comes about naturally, when they spark up a conversation, not the

other way around. Time to talk is on break, not at work. So, work, read, and write.

120. *"Cultivate humility and humanity." "Think of yourself less."* Words to live by, to strive for, to recognize the importance of to be real, to be human, humble, and equal to the rest of us. *Be human.*

121. Don't reveal too much too quickly, yet open enough to answer honestly – inspired by a good friend, E.D.T.V.

122. Remain indifferent to attention from others. You are not a kid anymore. It will get you nowhere but to an island too full of yourself. Accept self, accept ego, but refrain from holding on to the words others feed you, to the attention that others give you. You will be left alone on your island without food, nutrition, or attention to your needs. Instead, give yourself your own attention that you seek from other people. If we do this, we will satisfy our need to be attended to, will take care of our health and well-being, and be attentive to the workings of our minds, needs, and, in all, ourselves. *Well-being starts from you and in you, with you alone.*

123. You can be a hypocrite and still give out the greatest advice, but seek *not* to be a hypocrite – this is clear. Try to seek out a harmony in your words, thoughts, and actions. Seek out balance from the inconsistencies around and inside you for true harmony.
124. Never try to fabricate or fluff up your speech. Aim to speak as simply as you can so the other person or party may understand you completely. The aim of communication is understanding the other party, the other part of the whole picture you are missing. Fill the whole with interpretation and you receive falsity; fill the whole with asking questions and hearing someone out and receive the truth. Exit flattery and speaking like a fool. Be open; listen to the truth.
125. On graduation day, from a school or a chapter in your life, show your happiness. Be proud of your accomplishment on the inside understanding how much work was put into it, knowing your battle was worth the struggle to complete. On the outside, smile and be content with your fellow graduates or coworkers to be happy together at last.

It may seem as if it was nothing by the time it is over, but what time you put in to continue to graduation was more than merely writing assignments and commuting to school. You put the productive back in you. You figured the importance of relationships. And most important of the three, you have endured long enough to pass on the wisdom of following through, through any struggle, to its end, no settling for less, no reason for hurry nor lack of persistence due to stresses and eventual deadlines. You have come so far, from the first year to the last, and it is important to know that that was what it took to ultimately receive the final goodbye to a chapter in your life. More than a sheet of paper received or time spent together helping others, graduation is a testament to all you could accomplish with time and hard work. Congratulations, graduate. *Be proud of what you accomplished. You made it – your perseverance and mind.*

126. It may be demanding, but periodically reread these passages to revitalize memory. It will inspire action, speed, speech, and

thought to match their ideal with your reality. Continue writing. Just as important, continue to *read*. It will nurture your mind and encourage thought, which leads to speech, that leads to action, which leads to the well-being of both mind and body. Clarity in mind and body comes from well-being, and from well-being, peace and harmony. *Continue to read.* Demand this change, that thought, this action.

127. Never doubt your ability to find what you are searching for. The answers are always there for you when you keep a look out. Searching for something can be a slow and tedious task, but the reward is to find what you've been longing for all along. Keep your curiosity and eyes open, keep constant in your search, and keep your head up, looking up after falling the first few times. You will receive what you consistently search for, so, *keep searching*. Investigate, then you will receive, either knowledge, or what you desire to see.

128. Why doubt your ability to push through a situation? – because it is challenging? The

more you change through your experiences, the more you will know, will grow, and will show yourself the ability you thought you never had. Challenge yourself to do more for yourself, to do more for others – yourself first. Prove to yourself that you can do what you've been imagining, thinking, and dreaming. In turn, you will inspire others just as much as you find inspiration yourself.

129. Save yourself before you try to save another – that other needs only themselves to save.

130. You cannot help others if your intentions are focused on them only. Have the courage to understand your true intentions to help another: '*I see I have something that this other person lacks or needs. I can and will give it to them for assistance.*' Helpfulness is given to another once it is first developed in ourselves. Truth about our abilities to help makes the transition from self to another an easy one to make. Once we understand ourselves and our suffering, we can understand the positions of other people and what they may face day-to-day. That is compassion and

understanding – the way forward to help another.

131. The peace of mind of many first comes from the peace of mind of one. *Find peace in yourself by doing what you set yourself out to do – helping yourself and others, too.*

132. Eliminate bad habits and false views to transform them into what is healthy and rightfully true. Little effort will amount to greatness if you would only continue. It is up to you – your actions and views – to make what is given to you great, as what is great is truth. So, make yourself real, make yourself impersonal, abundant in truth, for your views, your actions, and your persistence will be the proof. Proof of what? – *the benefits of living well, actively, and true.*

133. Be mindful of your mistakes as you accept them as your own. You can do this in your mind with no need of explanation out loud. Simply correct what you have done wrong to others or to yourself. If someone else goes wrong, think to yourself: "*What if I had made this same mistake? Would I want others to*

condemn me, to look down upon me, to stare at me judgingly? So, why do you judge, look down upon, and condemn your own mistakes?" Practice this, and you will be all right by your mistakes. We are all imperfect, after all.

134. Acknowledge the truth: we are imperfect people in an imperfect world. Yet, there is a possible harmony in the imperfect people of our world. This harmony creates *perfection* in an unjust society by way of the just people it shelters. Being hospitable is always possible. In equilibrium, the negative and positive balance out – both those who are good and those who are bad are equal in stature and value.

135. In seven days, you have typed out over one hundred passages. In another seven, you can dish out another one hundred, too. You have made a consistent process successful, and can continue to make the consistent process successful, *if only you would continue*. Aim for the maintenance of gradual effort; its effect will be unanticipated and the rewards will be shown to more than you alone. Show

yourself to show others, too. *Do what you do – push through.*

136. Remain calm through facing your fears with courage, not fearlessness. Fearlessness is attained with *practice in* fearful circumstances. *'Scary' is not as strong when you show courage.* So, show yourself what you are worth, that you are worthy to *overcome*, then make peace with what you fear. Do not, however, put yourself in the way of fear – only deal with it when you must. When should you face your fear? – *when its opportunity is staring at you right in your own.*

137. Your mind is your home and your sanctuary. Make it clean, easy, clear, and bright. Cultivate your mind throughout every day and night.

138. Love the life you lead by choosing your own course and speed. Select the difficulties you take on and the choices you must make on your way. Enter the stream and tread lightly among the hardships you will come by. Know it's in you to face the challenges that you will soon come by.

139. Why try for **perfection** if we are imperfect beings? – to satisfy the good in us, to become better in a craft, to become better at being a human being? But what is important for this? What is the purpose to me? Is it more than for character, status, or identity, more than for a name, a body, a life? How about personal qualities, actions, and passions? What about humanity...? What about me? Heart and mind, body and consciousness, all just parts of a human being. Enduring? – no. Transformative? – yes. Ever-changing, impermanent, and imperfect for a reason – to come closer to the whole, to become one with everything else. Aim to *perfect yourself*, not to be perfect. The difference means all the difference in your world, in *our*

140. Deny yourself food when you can, deny drinks when you can, indulge when you can, excitement, entertainment, and pleasure when you can. Why? – true pleasure, true excitement, true joy is found in the untouchable, is had through expression, through speech, art, and connection; through the establishing of a new friendship,

rekindling of an old one, without expectation, we can find joy in our hearts and laughter all 'round. This is pure pleasure, not mere sensation; intangible pleasure, sense's cessation. It's our choice to choose the worldly or higher than our day-to-day; choose wisely to transform what you thought was the world's unchangeable way.

141. Remember the people you meet along your way. The words you speak place an imprint upon the mind. Once spoken, words do not go away. Only with making effort in the mind do they decay. *Allow the false words to drift away.*

142. Take your own advice when at a loss for another suggestion. It's up to you to think, resolve, choose, and sufficiently question. *Think, dammit, think!*

143. You cannot remember all your passages by heart, but you can trace them back through your memory. The contents of a mind ripen with meditation and connection with others, with nature, through yourself. Use time wisely and cultivate your connections to all four.

144. Quick, steady, consistent efforts are great accomplishments of human action. Calm, ready, and flexible efforts are those which strengthen mind and reaction. Act and react, find equilibrium in human action and reaction. Go forth and be prepared for the unpredictable as you move towards greatness... you will see that you will foresee the possibilities.

145. Rhythm, harmony, and silence in thought, stillness in movement, are spoken in wisdom's tongue. Trust your gut and guide with powerful precision; never compromise your principles to stay true to what you believe in. Believe in what you think, in what you say, and in what you do. Keep it within truth to cultivate wisdom and insight, too.

146. It takes great smarts to lie, but takes great wisdom to speak the truth. *Never cheat yourself. How so?* –speak your truth.

147. Do not work yourself up over petty things such as text messages or phone calls. They can be nice to receive, but need be no more than that. Do not expect any in return.

148. Do not allow yourself to force any situation

to occur. Find the right time and execute accordingly. The right time exists, and it's your chance to make it happen. Let it happen naturally, in respect to what is given, for the right reasons. *If it's not the right time, everything will be in its proper place, and there is no need to worry.* Relax and let life happen.

149. Seek to improve yourself, your situation, however far along your journey you may be. **Imperfection**: ever-more improvement; to make room to adjust to perfection.

150. Virtues are where my head and body will be when the important things in life are represented *by me*.

151. Meditations allow for flow, for letting go, for letting the mind trickle down its woes, for allowing the head not to explode. Fade into your breath to meditate mindfully. Happiness is the goal, solid in tranquility.

152. Physical endurance is not as important as spiritual endurance, although both are persistent efforts, ones which are naturally rewarded with the habit to continue. Long- or short-term, the rewards make your **will** more than willing.

153. Open your heart to openness, for yourself and others alike. You'll meet with precisely who you are, so make sure you're making yourself **true**. It's about who you've been, who you are now, and who you're becoming; it's simply you, so just relax, take care, and be mindful of yourself for you are all you need to be.
154. Endure physical pains, emotional pains, and mental disturbances. Persist while attempting not to complain. Strength of character is *not* attained in vain, it's how you'll go about the struggles that come to you.
155. Persist until the very end, with not much left to say; only those who are near to listen can hear the efforts that will come out of you. *You know what to say, so speak with action – words fall short of the markings of a deed.* So, let your deed be done for it to speak on its own accord.
156. Even when you're tired of trying, don't give up on your endeavours along the way. They will be there with you as everything else turns old and grey. Works come back 'round to you to show exactly what has been done.

Reap in the rewards of what you sow, and practice the best of what you know.

157. Thought manifests itself into the form of reality. Thoughts make great, powerful, fresh, and new. *Thoughts, with great thought, will come through to you.*

158. What is it that you write this for? Remind yourself. It is to remind yourself of your achievements in thought and action, using language to communicate what you know has worked and will work for you. Theory within the practice is important, just as the intentions are to the actions we choose. Look to yourself for inspiration since you are an ever-flowing fountain of knowledge to help you move – only be prepared to move with two feet on the ground. Accomplish what you know you can and make a difference in people's lives. Remember that you are a person, too.

159. Lead the life that you love through communication: from your actions, good deeds, with people, places, and things. But how would someone learn to live what they love? You must try, and then do. And then try

again on what fails, then do again. Then, if your trials lead to nowhere and they are not for any worthy cause – and you will *know* what a worthy cause looks like – try something else. Then, try that again until it works. And it will work. Trust me. But do not trust me if you cannot trust yourself.

160. Forget all of what I've written thus far. Know you are no more than your conscious awareness. Do not identify with your thoughts. Feel the connection you share with everything around you. You are part of everything and everything is in and around you. Be not afraid of a change in your consciousness, just be open to embrace the change of feeling, of mind, of perception. You are not your thoughts! You *are*. Period. We *are*. And we are *right here* and *right now*. Then, be here, and be now.

161. Try to understand all you should not do, should *never* do, and what to do, to *always* do, in your time and in various stations. Know how your mind works; do not feel discouraged about it since it is a part of your world. Your mind is a wonder. Feel its

magnificence when walking in nature, while the mind dissolves into one with what surrounds it. The mind becomes nameless and unidentified as all becomes one – you are just one part, and yet contain all in that one. Experience one. All you must do, is *be*.

162. Do not add to your plate when it is already full. Eat, digest what you've got, and feel satisfied with overcoming your hunger. You can overcome your lot by appreciating what you've got, for what you will receive is of benefit in the scheme of things.

163. I can keep going with what is available in the present moment; this will help when the present is out of mind in forgetfulness. Mindfulness is the opposite of forgetfulness. Being aware means to be mindful, to be fresh in what's here, and to make the moment count in usefulness with skill and effort. Yet, effort becomes effortless once a move is already made, once the ideas become real, once the present becomes past. Therefore, make each moment in effortlessness last.

164. **Determination**: to see yourself to completing your goals, coming closer to your dreams,

ideals, and plans. Planning is the action word; action is the substance of the plan. Make your life substantial. Move in harmony with your own determined actions. Determine what will happen by doing it – and what *could* happen, at that.

165. Nothing is lost; much can be gained.
166. Creativity flourishes in the mind, in the body, and in the spirit. We are human beings who need creation to fulfill our conscious desires. To bring something forth from seemingly nothing is to astonish ourselves and possibly those around us, making real what was once only imaginary. So, create what you will with intent and purpose in the direction of what is good. Benefit is to flourish as our creativity soars in its righteous place – in the world. Therefore, an outlet is required. *Find your outlet; create for life to happen.*
167. Do what is most ordinary first, first things for your body, for nourishment, as physical work. Then, for what is more complex, make it simple – think simply, write simply, speak so that others may understand. What is good for your body will also be good for

the mind, the area of highest priority. Use this method when making a list of priorities, *life* Set yourself up... for the ordered way. Prioritize!

168. Beauty is arranged in beautiful patterns, found among the ordinary and even the mundane. Look up the word – it means *worldly*. Cultivate a mind that can find life to be extra-ordinary even if you do not live extra-ordinarily. You don't need to be extra to live your life.

169. Try to stay away from people who are more interested in speaking about others rather than those who think about others.

170. Attempt to sway yourself from doing the wrong thing. The right thing becomes natural to do with constant practice, discipline out of the equation with habit in doing good. Discipline is not needed when practice becomes natural. Discipline is only needed when the wrong things take over your actions, your love, your life. Clear the way for yourself to live righteously in good actions. Then discipline becomes habit, while the habit becomes natural. Therefore, seek to be

a natural human being. How do you know what is a natural human being? – represent nature herself; do not force and only allow things to be.

171. Just as you do as you do when you are away from the regard to others' opinions – look to the world with the same indifference. Appreciate its beauty, the beauty of the world, in a detached manner, knowing it to be beyond your active control. Even towards those you love, be indifferent to their natural behaviours and tendencies, for they, too, are far out of your control. Any mention of reproach should be kept to yourself until a person crosses your path. In that case, first tolerate, and then, if necessary, educate the person on what should not be done, and what could be done instead. *Educate for the worth of another and yourself.*

172. The future could hold a harmony or hold disintegration. It is up to you to be part of its harmony or positive progression, or its disintegration and degradation. Connect, then, to yourself and to others with your *whole*

mind. Your whole mind is your attention, interest, and control of your actions – words and deeds. The future depends on your mind to sustain humanity and our various human endeavours. *Be clear with what you want your future to hold.*

173. Trying not to mess up? Do what you know is best to do, not what is a sorry attempt or a only second-best action of interest. *Do it*, and do *not* just think about it. Do *not* just plan. *Perform. Act.* Make things happen. With your choice of doing something, everything changes. You'll never know what may come through until you ***do.***

174. When you commit to something, make sure it is in your best interest. An expense of not doing so is to witness the unforeseen and negative consequences of your choice. What does this mean? – choose to be a surgeon, regret it after 2 of 6 years of schooling; choose to be a writer, regret it once people start critiquing what you write. Make sure you're willing, then, to face the consequences of your contemplated decision. Your choice

will be rewarding only once you think through the possible struggles, setbacks, and eventualities.

175. Listen, with your whole head and own two ears, to the person who is talking to you. Are they taking up time to release all their concerns onto you? – *listen*. Do not become distracted or question why they are telling you some revealing things right away. People need to unload, and some do so onto others. Work with it by paying attention to their words, feelings, and the implications of the facts of their stories. Their tone may imply they are distressed, worried, or anxious, so be supportive member of their community and listen intently and personally.

176. Anxiety is based on the future while depression is based on the past. Note the focus of the speaker and where they place their focus of time. Help them come back to the present to plan (for the future) and piece together the past.

177. Why worry instead of move on? Why complain instead of accept? Why hold on when

you can let go? *Why let go when you can hold on?*

178. Free yourself from overthinking what is past. Thinking of the past has its place, but the importance should be placed on coming back to the present. If you want to live life fully, if you want to make a difference in your life and in others', *stop worrying about what you have done.* Get on with it. Do what you must do to work, live, breathe a little easier, *without harming yourself or other people.* Make it harmless, seamless, and fruitful. Be the cause of someone else's smile. Seek out proper goals – this can mean completing a routine. Be present to live here one hundred percent of the time. You are capable. You are willing. And, *you can.*

179. Practice preparation. Organize your days into an ordered sequence, from first to last. If commuting, ask yourself: "Which places are closest to me that I can travel to first; which places should I go to on the way back?" Organizing yourself like this helps you to prepare for the ordinary dealings of

daily life. See the worth in your planning and consider your responsibilities, what needs to get done first, second, and last. Order is everything in a life full of possible disorder.

180. Give yourself a needed break after you have worked hard enough… although there is nothing sweeter than the experience of seeing your own limits being pushed successfully.

181. **Balance**: noting and working with all the various aspects of your personality. To give each facet its own due time is balance. Flexibility is putting on a role you are not used to with ease after a few failed trials. Adapting to a scenario with swiftness, grace, and flexibility will lead to ultimate success. Counter your anxiety with balance and flexibility – have confidence in these capabilities. Build balance up from underneath you into the energy inside of you. Do not be frightened – embrace the change of circumstance. Be brave enough, since everyone can, to change to embrace both the better and the worst. The worst will happen, yet the best can come (*out from you*).

182. Cultivate what you know is best and adapt it to more and more circumstance. Keep your cultivation fresh with its exposure to the present moment. Create a moment to flourish in your own attended time. This is to practice what you know is worthy of your time. *Make your time spent worthwhile.*

183. **Goals**: freedom, fluidity, flexibility, and flourishing. Find your own outlet, your own space, your own atmosphere, and explore the depths of experience both in and outside of your mind, body, energy. Possibility will open to not dry up. Bird, water, sway, endeavour. Keep your eye on the object of your mind. Then, be free, be fluid, be flexible, and flourish.

184. Let *what is* **be**. Do not influence what happens around you. You'll get your part. Your time will come up whether you see it or not.

185. Make yourself one with all you see and perceive. This is the only way to cope with your surroundings in harmony. *How do you do this? – you look at another as yourself.*

186. Face your fears by combatting the small ones first on your own or with willing others.

The real goal is to make peace with fear, not to fight it or bring it out to fight. But to overcome is necessary, lest you run the risk of fear overpowering you. Overcome fear, then, with facing it head on only to find the peace you weren't expecting, what you weren't looking for when you then get it.

187. *Turn yourself around.* When you are complaining in your head or out loud, not understanding why you are in the position you are in, remember the position is a temporary instance and will go away in time. Pick yourself up during these crucial times to free yourself from resentment or agitation. Times could be much worse, so pick yourself up. Turn anger around to calm. Turn fear into peace, even resentment into compassion. Pick yourself up and keep walking. *You may be able to pick up others along your way.*

188. You are much closer than you think – to your final goals, to better yourself, your truest form that you want to come about for yourself. Keep your hopes focused on what is happening, what has happened, and what could happen *realistically*. Do not hope

for more than life may offer you, although it may come up as an offering. Only work your way towards your goals despite their possible heavy appearance. Nothing more can be done than the work it takes to move you forward toward your final goal. A better self comes in time, and you'll be practicing, if not practiced already. A truer self comes with practice and patience. Here you are, yet there you will be. *Anticipate what you could be.*

189. **Thinking**: the active binding of the network in your mind; the way to ground yourself in rational reality. It is not as pure as awareness – of your surroundings, of your motives, of your thoughts – yet thought is essential to identify what is part of your world. It is essential to work on thought whenever you have the chance in public or alone. The contemplative life is no small matter and is the most appropriate way to live your life to its fullest. Think and be happy. Contemplate what is real within your life.

190. **Resourcefulness**: to make use of whatever you got to achieve your goal. Think, write

down, or work with whatever comes to mind or into your experience. Even if you don't write, think and remember what you are here to do: to *spread goodness, inspire others,* and *thrive in your life.* 'Life is meant for living', so make your life worthwhile with whatever you have got and have to do. "*How do you live?*" Be prepared to respond: "*Like this,*" and act. Let your actions speak for themselves, in love, in help, and even under distress within your control.

191. Go through with your plans and remember what happens afterward. What was successful? What *shouldn't* you do next time? You really have nothing to lose but your concerns. What to gain is to be heartfelt, sincere, stern when necessary, to show your smarts in action, and be as excellent in your conduct as your field(s) of endeavour.

192. Are you agitated? Are you feeling weak? Are you tired or hungry? Then show your strength to push through these small moments – even fragments – of your time. You should know their moments will pass. Wait until you can't wait no longer to make your

exit count, to go to find yourself a meal, to say what you can't say while someone else is talking. Be patient; practice patience. Be kind; practice kindness. Be temperate; *practice temperance*. These are all virtues you strive to own at first, but, in the end of your practice, all virtues will become your true nature. How does it sound to flow in constant virtue? *Impossible?* Virtues are made for human endeavour. So, *get a move on*.

193. *Forgive yourself for your mistakes*. This is not something you haven't heard before, it is something you must do to let go of all the things you have done wrong in the past. **Forgiveness**: a passage of time of letting go of resentment, which comes easier with acknowledgement of our own misdeeds and time.

194. Use your experiences as your guide for your betterment, to ripen your better intentions in the practice of better actions. Seize your betterment by moving through problems swiftly and calmly. You can find your solution, and all it takes is subtle movements ahead.

195. When was the last time you regretted to wait for something better? When you're in a long line for that fast food of yours, do you regret the wait once the desired item of food scrapes your palate? So, why do you complain when you know that being a good person means waiting a tad bit longer for your goals to be met successfully than in a short time? Don't you know that it will feel like no time once the wait is over and you have what you sought?

196. **Inspiration**: what people need from others or other sources to initiate and enjoy the pursuit of their life's endeavours. This calls us to **help** each other to reach that goal, to strive for what encouragement can offer to another person and ourselves.

197. Just as this book will tend to repeat the same (or similar) sayings, pieces of advice, life will repeat the same lessons, moments, and patterns that have already been spun out by your choices and behaviours. Recognize these patterns. Show yourself you have mastered yourself as they come up. Prove that you recognize these patterns by performing

your role accordingly. Listen. Speak. Wait your turn. Remove your ego from a situation. Smile back. Be the person *you* want to be. And do it again. And again. *And again. ... And again*. Until when? – until you are mastered.

198. Love is the beauty of a moment in happiness whether it is alone or with another you admire and care for. Those you love make you happy, make you laugh and feel a bit more free. Love those whom you love fully by spreading the natural gifts you possess: the ability to hug, kiss, smile, encourage, help, and heal from pain. Love is healing itself – it has the power to mend wounds and ameliorate troubling situations into less severe ones by the comfort of those you know. So, love, dammit, love! And love *more* than you are loved by another.

199. Notice how everything moves in a certain frequency, in a certain state, pattern, and has its own occurrence. How viscus is water? How solid is a rock? How fast are these cars passing by, and how suddenly do they slow down? After their movement and substance

are understood, you can now say that you know more about their changing and consonant nature than you once knew more any thought of it. Study the nature of things carefully, and know what they are, or what they definitely are not. Do not just rely on what others say about the things you have heard of or know but *explore them on your own*, with your own two eyes, and your one vast mind. *Understand and see for yourself.* Everything changes, or rather, not everything will remain the same.

200. Treasure yourself by taking care of yourself by your needs. Do you want to hurt yourself with a drink you know that has some harmful chemicals? Do you want to take a break from the work you know that is beneficial to your practice and goal? Do you figure that someone else will do all the work for you? Forget this. Move on with it and get out there for more work, for showing yourself exactly to the situation. Be prepared for showing yourself just what you have, just what you are capable of. As a wise man once said, "*I have never come across someone who*

lacks the strength to do so." So, *do so*, ACT, and thank yourself later.

201. I have something to do... so why stop till it's done?
202. "I don't feel like it." Then *act* like it. Do it instead of complain. Do not value an excuse such as: 'I'm not feeling like it'. You will not lead yourself anywhere, toward anything productive, worthwhile, or started up and accomplished.
203. Numbers are all around us, but are just measurements of things we really cannot grasp. If we could grasp the whole of our experiences, we would no longer value the symbols and signs we ascribe meaning to. Numbers would fall short of our reality as it is. Names would not hold as much significance as the way things really are. However, we use numbers and names because we are human, and that is what is needed for our understanding of things. Language, numbers, and names. All necessary, but do not hit the mark of truth – *they only point to its way*. (Moses, krs1, after the fact though).
204. First determine what you need to focus on

and what is not your need of focus. If your task is to focus on *the task*, look straight ahead to your hands. What do they hold, what are they grasping for, and what should they grasp for? Second, make note of why you are grasping what you are reaching for. Is it worth your time? Do you need to be going after something, someone, like that? What could you be doing instead? Third, be aware of your answers to such questions. Then, move back for the answer to the second. Then, move back for the answer to the first. The cycle is then complete.

205. Not necessary, and necessary. What is unworthy of our time? Greed, lust, desire for more, desire itself, delusion? Hatred? Anger? Jealousy? Despair? Dread? And worthy – what is worthy? – freedom, accomplishment, responsibility, joy, and peace. Do yourself one to envision your way forward into your life. All these are within our control if only we put a tiny effort into their destruction every day for such vices that hinder our natural human rights. What we desire should be *not to* What we should want should be the act

of *not wanting*. If we accept all that we have, and know we could lose everything at any time, then we will appreciate what we have the more easily to not even ask for more. Ask *for nothing*, then, and receive *everything – everything that you rightly have for now and of the world to offer*.

206. Love is a power beyond the lust for power. Compassion is an understanding more powerful than intellect. Intelligence is the knowledge of what is true and the vision of what could be. Pragmatism is the practical knowledge to bring one's vision to reality. Matter and mind determine creation. Thoughts flow into words that can flow into action. So, what are we to do? – simply: the first, then the second, and then the third.

207. Words are important for transmitting facts and figures, meaning and direction for others and oneself; actions, however, must necessarily follow from them. The only progressive changes that may occur in one's life are made through action. There is no other tangible way to excel in our endeavours within reality. Act, do, perform! Transmit

what is in your heart, head and mind – the only way to freedom from your inaction and to much better.

208. Name your transgressions and place them in the past. Understand what caused you to do them and what followed from your fault. Know what you did was wrong, but forget the looking down upon yourself. The way to humility is strengthening the power of goodness to make goodness the natural way to be. Humanity is good once you uncover and understand the bad; compassion is much easier this way.

209. Your mind is a world for yourself to discover. Do not think you must move to travel. Sit, lie, or stand where you are and start looking, not forward, but inside. *The way forward is from inside.*

210. *Thoughts lead the way to awareness*, but still do not hit the true mark. The truth is that we must understand things without words while using words to get by in our lives. Everything is in contradiction until we balance between two opposing forces – one extreme and the other. Positive and negative forces

need each other to exist and for us to exist. We need to trust the two to be in unity with the other without thinking that one is the better. Unite with your energy, then, to balance out thought into silence.

211. *However overwhelming things may be, do as some say and 'take one small step at a time.' Clichés can make real sense if you study them with application rather than disapproval.*

212. The world is not what you want it to be, but what you need – more simply, it's all that we have. Study, then, what you really need and move forever on forward toward your truest goals... only remember you do not have all the time in the world to accomplish them. Learn your needs as you start to live by necessity alone. Cultivate a simple living.

213. Forcing things to happen is a force you must overcome. The desire to control is controlling you. Let go of your own control over everything other than yourself. Move ahead to bigger and better things – for you and the people who matter. No one likes a control freak... no one including yourself. Although it shouldn't matter what people think of

you, you should still look on how to let go of the desire to control others, situations, or outcomes outside of your control. Do as you do without controlling what will naturally come about; you will turn things towards the better if you let people and events play themselves out.

214. Figure out how to do whatever you want with the thought of what is *natural* in the world, *not* what is *conventional*. Do not look to the majority as the example, but look to what is nature herself. Most people do not necessarily act naturally, but what *is* natural is necessary and will accord to its own consistent patterns and effects, ebb and flow. Go, then, into studying the idea of living harmoniously with nature. Figure what is good about the patterns of this world and its works. You will figure out these rhythms in time since they are causal, coordinated, and consistent. *Go on and study what happens naturally.*

215. Get out of your house and out into the world. What good reason were you waiting

from the start? – no good reason. Get out there, and *go see what's out there.*

216. Swim against the current when? – when the stream is calm enough to swim in it any way you can.
217. Try to plan for your future as if everything was up to you alone. Prepare for setbacks, yes, but search for what must be done to get things started up to move along.
218. A week away from your chosen field of endeavour helps you to become more original with your ideas. Away from the actions you tend to perform helps you to keep things fresh and new in your daily life. Take a break, then, from yourself, your tendencies, your fears and concerns, to observe how it is to live a little more differently from your norms and tendencies.
219. Strive to live a better life. How do you do this? – make note of what you do in a day; now, scrap that and start off your day the way you want to. Wake up early, eat and shower well, meditate at least 10 minutes, take a walk outside, enjoy a book in your

own backyard (when the weather is accommodating), take a drive to buy a favourite flavour of coffee, and spend time with those you love, admire, and care for. Take a chance to do something new like these actions or others you prefer to do. See what happens and how happy you feel. The time is here to do it now. What do you really have to lose? – *I will tell you.... Without consideration of what consequences will spring from your actions, expectation of potential failures is not prepared for. Did you ask why you should drive just to buy a coffee you don't need to buy? Did you ask yourself why you should 'see what happens' instead of taking the sour and sting out of any situation, meditating on the worst-case scenario beforehand?* This practice is not meant to harm but to prepare someone for the worst case in order to deal with anything, and that means *anything*, that could happen. Once you are prepared, and *fully* prepared, you will then see how happy you can really feel. When you prepare, and do the right things, you will be happy.

220. If what you have got to lose is *time*, then

consider that time is out of your control. You can plan your actions or let time take up the best from you. You could wing it, use your natural instincts, or **plan** for your upcoming times ahead. What is best? – that depends on the reasons you give. You are the judge of your actions that make the best out of the time you will spend. Time will be spent anyways, so why not attempt something outside of your comfort zone? Don't allow time to waste you away; waste none of it and make your day.

221. Exercise daily. If not your body, then your **mind**. if not your mind, then your speech. If not by expressing, then by sympathizing. If not by sympathy, then by observing. You simply watch, at that point, and then learn. *Exercise how you learn, and do so every day.*

222. Do you have something to say? Do you think it's important, so important that you would interject in a conversation between other people? Well then, guess what? – it is not as important as you think. You can wait for the proper time to say what you need to say. Your turn will come up; if it doesn't,

it was not that important anyway – maybe a blessing in disguise. If it was important, then there would be a space in the conversation open to the opportunity for you to speak your mind. But there wasn't... so let it go. *Listen more than you speak and see what happens. You can thank me by trying it out for yourself.*

223. Enjoy being alive. How is that possible? – first, wake up. Then walk. Sit. Stand. Listen. Hear someone out. Speak. Walk away. Move around. Touch someone you love. Hold them. Take care of them, yourself by doing so. Wait, then see. Look around you and understand that almost everything you see is out of physical reach but not the mental hold of your mind. Be whatever you really are. And, most importantly, smile at it all.

224. You are you – most simply put, no one but your own self. Yet we are *selfless beings*. How does this work? We have our own bodies, dispositions, past tendencies, and upbringing. No one individual is the same as anyone else. Yet we are *selfless*. What does this mean? – we are connected to everyone and

everything in our world; we could have been any other person in the world, yet we are our own unique bodies and minds; we share an existence with other people and are interdependent; not one of us human beings could exist without all other living beings – humans, insects, plants, animals, and all that is found in nature. So, what are we? – we are selfless people in need of others to exist. This, considered, then, means no one individual being could come into exist without other beings. And, most astonishing of all, *we all happen at once.* What do we take from all this? – allow all things to happen naturally as your connection to all, as a human being.

225. Do you have the perseverance to read long passages? I hope you do. If not, here you are. But, for next time, challenge yourself: *choose a long one.*

226. Independence means to hold on to your own perspective after hearing out another person's words. You change what you direct your mind to, or what your perspectives are, with your own independent reason. This does *not*

mean to do things your own way and disregard other people and their perspectives. Listen then assess a situation, *independently*, with thought, reason, and judgment. Be a sculptor, not the lay of stone.

227. Disguise nothing in your speech. Speak freely to those you care about, even to those you don't like, who ask questions. Truth should prevail in any given situation. Do not hamper yourself from the truth. Embrace truth fully and recognize its beauty as pure freedom from what is false. *Freedom from what is false, corrupt, and delusional – freedom from fear – is the freedom of our own truth.*

228. Stick by your friends at *all* given expenses of your own. Never let go of those you come to know well who are naturally as valuable as you are. Make a constant effort to see your real friends at any given time when needed. Make some time to settle down with your companions, your brothers! Nothing is better in this life than friendship, affection, and working as a member of the larger community we call life.

229. Why did that person give me a stone-cold face back after I looked at them? The better question: does it matter to me whether they reacted differently than I expected? – nope. Will my outlook change their character? – not really. Should I give these facial expressions any second-thought? – listen: *control your own reactions.* Change *your* facial demeanour. Be kind and smile back to others, no matter how someone might react or not. Be true and be kind regardless of how they look or what they say – the takeaway for the day.
230. Avoid excessive speech. Talk calmly and gently. There is no need to cause a scene or ruckus or fight. Relax. Let it go. Speak freely. Expressing yourself is easy... with practice. So, practice and see for yourself what comes out of your mouth into the ears of another.
231. *Sensitivity is a gift bestowed to you.* Make use of your abilities and feel deeply.
232. There is no stopping you when you know you have the right idea. Now, get out there and go get onto your ideas.

233. Love the life you lead. Yet live your life by following. How do you do this? Instinct, nature, and reason: three guides for a great life.
234. Drop off your baggage to fly high above the ground.
235. Embrace the unknown since it will soon become the known, *if only you would dare. Dare, but with a calculated risk. Do what you were scared of doing once before.*
236. Listen to your feelings after your reasoning rather than your justifications. The reasons overcomplicate the raw feeling of intuitive knowing. Instinct is always a reminder. Be true to it and see, but never sidestep your reasoning abilities.
237. How do you free yourself from worry? – free yourself from all that does not really concern you. Then you will be much freer, lighter, and confident in your focus.
238. Even when angry, notice your own anger to eliminate any possibility of outburst. Remember that all emotions are transitory and able to be tamed.
239. When at a loss for words, stop talking. Trust

your inner guidance system, your intuition and good sense. *You know better, and much more, than you think.*

240. Reorder what is out of place in your life to begin to prioritize. Family, work, friends. Love is most important of all. *Love requires loving people – family and **all***

241. Come off as arrogant and no one will like you. Come across as humble and kind – people will come near. Be soft, be supple, and be gentle and true. There is no need for rowdiness or noise. *Tame yourself with everything that you feel.*

242. Do what you must to succeed in this world without harming anyone or anything. Do not think, however, you will get ahead without failing. You must fail and push forward to succeed, and you must continue through failure and learn from those mistakes: the unavoidable pains with an inevitable end.

243. What is your stance on politics? – you don't have one. Then, stay out of its conversation. *Know when you should say nothing at all.*

244. Why do you moan and groan when you

could get up, walk away, and move on? You cannot walk away? Are you certain? Have you tried? Are you *sure*?

245. Perfection is attainable only through accepting what we now have and what we are now. We are on the way to it, this perfection of ours. Live through acceptance to see how perfect we can be.

246. *Freedom is found in personal principles applied to your daily life. Principles are found in ideals to pursue. Ideals are what we strive for. Ideals are what can, and should, be real. So, love, trust, honour yourself and make peace with what you strive for. Be beautiful just as you are. And always, always, **always**know you are loved in return even as you fail at first tries.*

247. Never mind about what people say about you. You know you're a hard worker, and you work it well. What if someone disagrees? – prove them wrong by working anyway.

248. What is there to say that is so important that it must be written, spoken of, or expressed? Why, only those things which deserve proper attention out of urgency. What is urgent? –

what else but the discipline of exercising our rights and freedoms, of knowing what acting freely with our rights means, and the importance of acting as rational and social human beings? What is there to do but send out our knowledge to people who are readily willing to hear (*or read*) about a wisdom for our time? Philosophy could be one of our missing hubs to a more satisfactory life of joy; understanding, compassion, and humanity need a voice and some action, some thought for and awareness of our health and our progressive goals. So, we must take such a moment in time to devote some of it to the freedom of expressing our natural curiosity of activity, to go where we have not yet had the courage to go once times before. Let us make our way toward prosperity, virtue, and freedom, and into our rights that are natural for us to soar.

249. Why is it so difficult to read such a long string of words? Reading becomes difficult when one is restless, in a hurry, or overwhelmed. Calm yourself down to get back

to what you'd love to learn. Read what you've wanted to read – just *look* and *use your time wisely*.

250. Are you scared of change, of changing into what is truly on your mind to do? Remember that you will only gain peace once your mind and its corresponding actions are in complete cooperation and harmony with one another. Determine what is conducive to your health, for the benefit of living with and around others, to live your best part in life, the part that is meant for living.

251. Logic can be clear-cut if it is put in simple form, although there are times when you need space to logically sort some things out. There is no fault in taking time to make the right decisions or to choose your proper actions accordingly. Planning requires time, patience, and sometimes even silence. Libraries are beautiful places where silence can be used in its right place. So, find the time to test out your logic in a library: simply state what must be done and what else must be done for its completion. It's up to you to move to the right space to take your time to

decipher and choose. *In silence, you can find your centre.* Read, write, and *think*.

252. Rush or hurry, it's your choice, but leave it up to your effort and your own will. Do not force things; do not do for the sake of another, but for yourself first; see the worth in your own actions and limit what is done for the sake of profit, selfishness, and greed. Do for others, but not to the extent that you do everything they ask of you without proper judgment. Have a head on your shoulders and not the world and its people. **You alone decide what to do.**

253. Fun *is* all fun and games until you've reached its healthy dose... and there is *always* a limit for everyone; the best part: you get to choose your own. There are limits to everything that is good or pleasurable for you to show everything that's worse. Accept this and cut up your time into work, play, rest, and space; you will then learn the time and your own proper time and pace.

254. Listen to the words of others, but do *not* implement *all* you hear. The words handed down from others are **not** all sage pieces

of advice; some are just words without experience for their validation. Use your own judgment and own mental tools. Discover your truer good sense, the unique wisdom found within you. *Do not shun what's good for you.* Do not hide from saying someone is wrong.

255. Am I anything to you but words on a page? For what does it matter my status, background, or history? Is not 'advice for life' enough to provoke your curiosity?

256. Are you comfortable in your seat? Does it matter when everything around you pushes you to summon up your strength or endurance? What does it matter to be comfortable when events could be so much worse? *Look towards duty, not towards comfort, to get by.*

257. When at a time of feeling uneasy and imbalanced, work with some ways to counter a lack of harmony. Compose yourself in work or activity, or sleep or meditation. Creative fields may help, but do not overexert yourself. *Learn your true limits from the experience and influence of moderation.* Then, you know

how far you can go from how far you *should
Push a little further and you'll be surprised.*

258. Pleasure can be overcome with mind to reason over whim. True limits on pleasure require testing and balancing, not looking to others' experiences. What is a suitable meal? What is a healthy mean of living? Make up your own mind to matters of food, sex, travel, and worldly satisfaction. There is a spiritual limit set in place – for you – to help you not to falter; that spiritual limit is *you*, and your *choices*, and your *experience*.

259. Why do you concern yourself with appearances, the appearance of what people think about you? Why does it matter so much? – because reputation remains important. Change this frame in your mind: reputation means nothing except for the content of the minds of others. There are only few matters that *do* mean something to you most importantly, so learn and live them well – physical appearance to keep up with time; healthy body (cleanliness and exercise); to look good, for yourself and the sights of

others – are all that should be thought about when thinking of appearance. *Respect what you and all other people can see.*

260. Have some heart, some direction, some feeling towards what's good. What is good? Compassion and understanding others' perspectives and situations in their lives. How does it feel to be a housewife, a servant, to take on the role of a leader? How, in your body and mind, would you feel if you lost a relative, a loved one, a friend? – if someone broke your heart to shatter your expectations of the goodness in others? Learn to know that others have their battles that they are not willing to share; trials and tests up against them, it is **your job** to *understand*.

261. Too much heart is not ever too much, for so little is it openly found. Open yourself to love and abundance – it may keep you alive in and out. Only guard against those who will shatter your heart and see to it who and when one will tear it out.

262. Think and communicate moderately; think in real terms. According to the situations you have straight in front of you, communi-

cate in an open way. Truthfully, with respect and understanding, do not think of what is fantasy. You make your thoughts real and take your ideas into reality.

263. Do not speak in a derogatory language; be aware of the perceptions of other people. Would you want to be spoken to with foul language, in a demeaning tone of voice? – that would cause hurt and pain to another... would you want that for yourself, too? Speak in a soft tone, then, without enunciating any attention towards yourself. You will be better off, left in peace with speech and left in your gentle mind.

264. "Know your limit, play within it" works only if you have limits. Set them up for yourself.

265. Lying is the epitome of a failure in a devout spiritual life. When you speak the truth, you will be set away from the troubles of delusion and doubt. Do not play with words as if they were mere rules of a game. Look at words as solid structures that can bend or break other people. Throwing stones at others only causes harm, likewise throwing fits. Trust your truthful words, and use them

with your discretion. The truth can harm as well, so choose when to open up in time.

266. Pleasure and pain are a part of the same spectrum. If you avoid the spectrum altogether, you avoid the turbulence of pursuing one and avoiding the other. Avoid pleasures and pains and do what is right instead.

267. To show friendliness should be the goal of any interaction firsthand. Friendship can be as simple as showing interest in a person who you are near. Your interest can give someone an opportunity to be open with someone else, just as it gives you the opportunity to listen and hear someone out. Try and be open in speech and open to listen in all social situations.

268. Control your emotions; let them pass away as naturally as they come about. All emotions are temporary and none will last for long. Remember they are temporary in times of anger, frustration, pain, sadness, restlessness, or despair. *Grab the handle of your emotions to drive within your own control.* It cannot harm to ease up on your burdensome emotional load.

269. If you have access to the internet, you have a resource to search for whatever you want to learn. Make great use of this resource and see what comes back to you – knowledge, wisdom, laughter, insight, the world, or yourself. Whatever you do, *search wisely*; products you search for plant seeds in your mind and grow, but only subconsciously. Therefore, you must plant cautiously and consciously before you set out to know.

270. Keep things professional between you and the people who you interact with. What does *being professional* mean? – to keep a distance away from people that prefer space; to be diplomatic with people whom you work with or serve at work; to remain civil with those who you'd rather not talk to at all. Begin with being kind, reserved with people you don't know, polite yet private in public places. Show yourself how professional you can be and see that respect come back to you as well.

271. *Place your priorities straight.* What do you prefer to do in your time? Does it match what you would prefer to do if you listed

them as your priorities? Try this now: work, family, going out with friends, reading and writing, what is most important? – family. What means the most to you apart from this? – work, reading and writing, and going out with friends, in that order. Do you see yourself loving all four of these areas of your life? – of course. So, make time for them and do not succumb to laziness or inaction in regard to your priorities.

272. *Intuition and creativity go hand in hand.* Flow with what comes to your mind in creative endeavours and work with them all the way through to their complete works of art. See what results when you use what you must to continue your pursuit of creation, mainly, with creativity and intuition. *Create with a mind that is wide, awake, and aware; it is the condition of your best work.*

273. How do you balance professional work life with entertainment and playfulness? – during moments of conversation with people, pick a quick remark to spark a laugh or smile both for the listener and yourself. Mesh work life with a playful life and teach

yourself how to be both: serious at one time, while being joyful at the other. Do what you have to do, but make it fun for yourself, too. *Take life seriously – but not **that**seriously.*

274. Instinct, creativity, logic. You can put all three of these into harmony together. Use your instinct to guide your words and actions, creativity in your solutions, which is resourcefulness, and logic in your thought, with instinct in action. Logic requires an eye to action paired with diligent thought, both which compose practicality. With practice you make reason *real*, no longer *ideal*. *Follow your instinct and reason it out step by step. Use your mental and physical resources creatively. You will find answers to the questions that bog you down and leave you guessing.*

275. Numbers matching, stories relating, scenario after scenario of recognizable patterns are **coincidences**. Nothing is there for a reason and nothing is here for a reason. Yet we create the reasons. We choose how to understand them. Someone could tell you how to understand, but *you decide* whether you agree or disagree. Remember your independent

mind here. We can relate to people with the coincidences we share and can talk about similar interests there as well. The meaning we create is that coincidences are used for initiating conversation or a sense of connection with others. I make up the meaning, yet the meaning is *not made **for*** me; it is ***from*** me as I create it myself.

276. Everything happens for a reason? Nothing falls short of synchronicity? Everything is connected and intertwined? Therefore, everything happens for a reason? Everything *is* The past came before the present and the present flows into the future. Reasons are man-made, work with logic, and could work through experience if you gave it the time of day. *However*, reasons are created by rational *and* irrational people. Someone could argue that everything happens for a reason, but only because they are a human being, and people **have to** have reasons to understand. Using rationality is how we function in a free society. Therefore, everything happens for a reason *of which a person determines themselves*... or in a group... or as a follower... or

leader. If you determine things for yourself *every time*, you fail to be a follower. You lead yourself and for yourself *alone. You* make yourself and *you* are the reason. So, reason out why you will think as you do, then move on.

277. *People may challenge you throughout your life. Create* the reasons why. What could the reasons be? – to make you wise for your age, to strengthen your character, to prepare you for the your life ahead of you, for what you will be 'destined' to do. I take the third road, then the second, and then the first. Destiny is what you make of it, so give it the best of what you got.

278. Be considerate of those who are around you. Do not judge people for what they look like at first glance – that is merely judgmental and base, which misses the substance of a person's worth and true character. Consider yourself worthy enough to consider other people, *but don't forget to consider yourself first.*

279. *Eat when you're hungry, cease when you're full.* Take this in when watching episodes of T.V., spending time on the internet, and, of

course, when eating – especially with company. The object of your cravings will not satisfy as much as the sensation of delayed gratification. **Life gratifies naturally** – *remember this.*

280. Do your work, then let it go: this is the way. And it works; *try it out and see.*

281. You do not always have to conform to what others do – *and you shouldn't* – but when you do, keep up with the natural order of the scene. You do not disturb the peace when you conform to what is natural within a group, as in keeping silent when sitting in a lunchroom or eating silently on a work break. Interrupting the silence is a bother and disturbance to others who are attempting peace and calm, so, avoid disturbing the peace with your very best effort. *Only go against the grain when you see the grain's harming another.*

282. Amazing amounts of energy? Perfect style in mind? Is it true? or is it a figment of your imagination? Maybe you need some grounding, maybe something a bit more calming. Maybe it is a slice of humility you need to

digest. You may have to remember you are only one of billions of small networks of particles in this life that not everyone knows or will know or hear about at all. You may not even know yourself. So, humble yourself down to size, to the part of the world around you.

283. Be nice, not a flatterer. There is harsh judgment behind all praise – *influenced by Tolstoy.*

284. Trust your gut, not what somebody tells you. "Fact" may just be an opinion. Opinion is subjective, so take that into account often. *Objectivity comes from disregarding everything that's personal and transforming it into what's im You think you can handle that? – you could with time and trust.*

285. The people in our world can be cruel, all for themselves, exactly what you see them to be. Don't forget in times of talk with bad subjects that goodness triumphs. Any form of mischievousness is out there in human beings. Humble yourself to know, however, that you could have fallen trap to those same ill-intentions, too. Stand up for yourself in front of what you seem to oppose from

your character, but know what your character could have been without your effort in goodness.

286. Experience tells all. Don't rely on only what others say. Look and see for yourself. There is no harm in double-checking what is said by others, as it is a form of analysis and proof for yourself alone. Rely on yourself and *only those you know you can trust. Those people you trust are those that love you and other people unconditionally – a possibility.*

287. Don't play yourself by trying to be super cool, super good, or extra kind. Just be cool, good, and kind. That is all, and it's as simple as that.

288. What to do on the two hundred eighty seventh day of the year? Make a plan for the next day, next few days, or simply just today. You don't have to plan everything – 'everything' you have no control over – but you can plan for everything that is *under your control*: place, time, choice, and long-term goals. *Set goals and prioritize what's in your power. What is in your power? – your mind and all it can do.*

289. Enter a maxim, a law, a rule unto yourself to do only what is good and that which is true. Lies need to be vanquished, truth is to be the rule. You always own your actions, so you must own up to what's good and true. *Make action your priority in goodness and in truth.*
290. *Breathe in. Think. Breathe out. Walk. Breathe in. Look. Breathe out. Listen.*
291. Taking a walk out in nature brings you back to the earth. *Where were you before?*
292. When things don't work out when you want them to: do not force, do not complain, do not be dissatisfied, do not worry – these are things you can control. Do what you can do and the rest will settle through, *but do **all** you can do, and see yourself to it through and through.*
293. If reality is just a dream, why not make it dreamlike? Why create our dreams in reality in the first place? What is stopping us from shaping our visions into reality, to make our dreams come true? The answer: our reality has limitations, physical at the least. What do we do with them? – that is up to our imagination to work with for our making.

Dreams can come true, but only if they could become true in our reality. What is real? – that which is tangible, intelligible, and what we can see, sense, and feel. What is unreal? – superstition, lies, and projections of character. Sidestep those three to make what you want to see, what you want to think, what you want to feel *real. Make your reality real.*

294. Anxious energy passes through a medium to be handled and controlled, to be maintained as a healthy energy and not as depreciating. Answers to find a healthy medium: reading, writing, dancing, singing, looking at a piece of art, listening to music, talking – any medium that may allow you to become absorbed in something other than yourself and your problems. *Take a break from your problems and master your craft,* **a** *Who knows, you may even use creation to treat your problems.*

295. Waiting is a game that must be played. The game is simple: you could either be beaten, or you could triumph. You must use your patience in doing nothing for a temporary moment of time. To win this game, you must know that every passing moment is

temporary and that nothing lasts forever. Therefore, all our times of waiting will pass and we will go on about our day as if nothing long ever happened. As if there were nothing to wait for, start to act, *and wait*.

296. Darkness changes to light as light shines through darkness. Evident? But how does **someone** shine? Not through abrupt comments or loud noises, but through truthful words, good deeds, and silence once words are spoken, once deeds performed. You shine when you act through character, your goodness, with nature, and through time. *It's your time, so make it shine*.

297. Most things have already been said; there is no need to repeat unless someone doesn't already know. Do not repeat yourself to those who already know, repeat yourself to those who fail to understand the first time. *Repeat yourself to yourself after you get it the first time*.

298. Lead the way for yourself through *your* actions, not those of others. You should not conquer anyone, but should conquer your ill-conceived actions and self-depriving tendencies – smoking, drinking, excessive

living. Lead the way by making an example of yourself to what is good in you. Know your good place and aim to stick by it.

299. Stick to what you do regardless of who happens to be around you. You are the driver in the seat of your choices and attitudes. Do not let this burden weigh on you; simply let go of what others think of you and do what you would do naturally *as if no one were to judge you*. Only then can you find confidence in your choices, in each one of your actions, *whether in public or in private*. Just make sure to consider people and their loads along your way.

300. Be civil with the people you dislike. Say hello to the people you judge too quickly and offhandedly. Practice non-judgment and cultivate a real liking for all sorts of people you see and interact with. You cannot get by peacefully without some practice in civility.

301. Warm yourself up with the clothes you wear, not to seek designer clothing for appearance or status. Both are a waste of valuable money, money that could be spent on more important matters, such as people, education,

expenses, and sustenance: for food, shelter, entertainment with others, **a life**. Choose the products and consumables you purchase wisely. *Beware of indulgence and the pursuit of material goods.*

302. Everyone has something they've always wanted to say to someone. What better place to express what was never said in person than on paper or in your head, even aloud when in private? *Prepare* – in your head, on paper, or out loud – *for the best you can really do.*

303. Who am I to say the things that I say with any authority or conviction? Am I someone special, someone you must listen to to live your life wisely? Do I consider myself someone smarter than anyone else to tell you how to live your life? **Not at all**. I simply have much to express although still I have much to know and, more, a ton to still figure out for myself. However, in the moment, how lovely it is to feel that someone might get something out of whatever I give away, or do, or say, or *think*, or *feel*, or **write**.

304. Put others' needs before your own for a

difference. See what it feels like to be selfless before you condemn someone for 'trying to be a hero'.

305. You *can* ignore the things that do not concern you and still live your life satisfactorily. You can even smile at the nice fact that you don't have to worry about the things that do not affect your life. Do this, I ask of you, for drama not to follow you, disasters not to burden you, for you to be settled into your own directed aims and ambitions according to your own business and *not the affairs of others*. Focus on you and what you must do. Then let the rest come along as naturally as night turns to day – naturally outside of your control.

306. Stick to the sticky situations you find yourself in and take your time to step out of them. If it is your problem, take it as a duty to figure your way out of it, *not around*. Invest your time **in** your problems, yet have the intelligence to step **away** when you have had just about enough. You will tend to have an instinct when enough is enough;

however, see how long you can keep at it. *See how far you can go.*

307. Keep steady and at your own pace. Others' effects on you work against you only if you allow them to. *You* allow them in. Remember you can think about your actions and control them on your own time. *Have the power to maintain some composure and guide yourself alone, when- and wherever you may be.*

308. Finish what you have started …as simple as that. The exception: a perfect mistake.

309. *Grand accomplishments come from small beginnings, simple actions, and small, simple efforts. Therefore, make your works great by taking them little by little. Wait for a moment to be precise in what you need to do for the next step. Take on the challenge of making yourself a grand statement, a great proposal, a great, grand **life**.*

310. *What about this writing is appealing to me? Is it that it will gain me praise for being so different from others? Are there reasons why I should continue other than living by the principle of completing what I start? Maybe the purpose of this book will come closer to its end, closer to its*

true purpose, to know that praise will get me nowhere. Or maybe it is a way to come to insights about my own mind, how it has been affected by the readings I have read, the thoughts I have culminated, the language I have learned through experience, books, and communication. Maybe I have some answers to very general problems, maybe I am trying to be profound, or I may be simply the product of my environment and all the tiny parts that compose it. Maybe – just maybe – I will look to the depths of these writings and notice the themes that hold center in my life, the eccentricities in my head, and the further reaches of my mind that I have never yet known until the buttons I type are pushed one by one. The words I write move through my hands up to my eyes to see – to see what but myself? Here, I can finally witness at firsthand, the truth. And so, **I write**.

311. Notice what's around you right now. Go ahead, look around. Do you think someone is watching your every move? Do you do things to draw attention to your conduct? Do you attend to what is around you at all? Do you even need to? *There are times when*

*I feel as if someone is watching me, yes, but I look around to see people attending to their own business. Yes, I have thought of drawing attention to myself and gain some sort of reaction from others, as I attend to people's perceptions. And yet, I've seen that I only need to focus on what is at/on/**in** my very hands, what is directly within the focus of my immediate experience. How could have I been so blind not to see my mind's eye peak from its awareness? I can note the silence of my surroundings and tune out the clutter that is within my head, slowly to retreat into a deeper state of mind in the silence which surrounds me. Now, I see what is clear and immediate: my emotion, my depth, and myself; I see my attention diverted to what is happening all 'round and inside.* So, I **look around**.

312. Does coffee stimulate your mind enough? To do what you should be doing, you must drink coffee? Being productive, that is, is what you should do. But what if all you need is some focus of mind instead of the coffee you drink, an effort to develop the concentration of your mind, and the energy you get from everyday food and water to

keep up the current of awareness on your work and natural life? Maybe this is the answer you have been looking for, as it is at **your disposal** if you truly search for it – in your mind, your hands, your lips, ears, body, vitality. Focus, and you will achieve; direct your energy, and you will find a cure (to forgetfulness). Wake yourself up to the layers of 'right now': no coffee, no stimulants required, but only nature and the motions of experience all around.

313. Look deeper inside to refine your mind. *Think directly and clearly.* But how? – *read on.*

314. Choose wisely. Feel out your choices with your reasons as they come to you. Seize the best that is in your hands or your head, whatever's at your disposal right now. Prepare for the worst and act towards the best. Do not fool yourself with trickery or deceit, foolishness or lies, even covering up for yourself to do otherwise. *Be true!* With yourself and your options, be true – this is the far best you can do.

315. See the goods that you have, especially when

they are right in front of your eyes and in any direction.

316. Remember it is okay to miss out on some days where you could have been a bit more productive, especially when it comes to spiritual practices such as meditation, or physical practices like working out. Forgive yourself and let go of your lack of initiative. Move on by doing more with your time. Direct yourself to the path you find most suitable for you and go, go, go! What's suitable for you? – what you are inclined to do when you happen to be free.

317. Think, man, think!

318. How can I cultivate better relationships with people, a healthier connection with people, and proper conversation? *I could be more friendly, more kind, more generous with what I got and what I have, letting go of the idea that my belongings belong to me.* Belongings are out there for any person to hold to for a time, accept, then give away. Therefore, even all ideas can be anyone's to hold for a short period of time before they are

given away to those who are more deserving. Give freely, then, and accept the offerings of positive, powerful ideas. Give gifts of the mind; they are as good as or better than the material satisfactions we slave to in our heads. Give and receive! – this is the power of our action.

319. Do not let silence bring you down. Do not accept silence as awkward, weird, or strange. **Embrace** Accept a person, place, or scene just as you can accept yourself. If you need some help to accept yourself, *read this book!* Understand that others share your perspective and have more to share with you. Silence in between a scene may become more substantial, enduring, and open for more room to be free in your shared time. *There is freedom within the silence.*

320. Fantasy, freedom, and imagination have their limits – necessary and practical limits. This is required of you to tame each at your own expense, for your own sanity and your own shared reality. This process happens slowly but time, focus, and strength of mind *are*

required to free you from your delusional ways of mind. Be free within limit to do what you know, to know what you must learn what is real and what is good, what is just and true. Then, let freedom and imagination be your fuel, your *creative* fuel to create *a world of your own*.

321. When you feel something out of the ordinary, do not allow it to overwhelm you. When you feel out of sorts in your mind or body, fix your mind upon your thoughts and feelings. Recognize them by name and learn to know them for yourself and your own levels of comfort. Then, and only then, can you know to recognize yourself. You are not yet what you want to be, but *already have everything you need to be*. Only practice is required of you to make yourself what you want and what you need to be more **real**.

322. Words are merely sounds, and yet, with meaning, are more powerful than ever thought imagined. However, actions influence truth. Influential words and actions are, then, a cause for harmony and peace

in the body and mind **when acted** upon in truth. Act upon your truth and, for once and all: **live**.

323. Words and actions in discord cause stress, despair, and uneasiness. Therefore, we must learn to be in harmony with our words and actions. You will have your share of peace in the world within your mind and body. One step further: place yourself in an environment where words and actions are held dear, uphold to truth and goodness and peace. It is here, in peace, that you will thrive on what is good and banish what is deceitful, greedy, fearful, and forgetful of your goodness. Concentrate on what is just, on what is pure, on what is good – truth speaks, and it is dependent on action.

324. Going into isolation does not mean you will be lonely necessarily. Living on your own, however, does not mean that you are necessarily strong. Retreating to move away from your problems only escalates them. Growing away from your family does not decide maturity; what decides your maturity is clear thinking. Thinking for yourself determines

your strength of mind. You decide your maturity and you decide what is best for you. To grow away from family will make you appreciate; to grow together will make you strong together in time with effort from each party. What you choose is what's important: do you want strength, gratitude, or safety? *Choose wisely*.

325. Superstition is unnatural. What is required of us is to follow what is natural. *Naturally follow the natural*.

326. *Just finish the page*, I say to myself in the silence of my kitchen as the clock strikes 12:20 in the morning, hands reluctant, 'no' as their answer. *Reach the end of the line, **then** take your deserved break*, is what I say to myself, thinking about quitting early, thinking of other things I could be doing instead. *Breathe now*, I say, *I'm headed to satisfy the goal of my choice. No turning back now*, as I reach for that final statement. And here you have it: *my passage*.

327. Love and luck can break you in half, so here are some ground rules for destroying the destroyers: *Rule 1*, write out your expectations;

Rule 2, crush them on your own time, on your own sheet of blank paper, or in your own mind; *Rule 3*, do not let that stop you from the hard work of loving the luckiest thing our life has to offer: our love itself. Luck comes from hard work. Love comes from support, joy, giving and belonging. Bring **hard work** and **giving** together and what do you get? The luckiest reward with no exception: love and all of its glory.

328. Just get to it, now. You don't have all day, only a select amount of time. *What are you waiting for?!* Shatter those expectations of yourself and get out there.

329. Music from the 'soul' should not be tamed …but what is a *soul*, anyway? Maybe just a void, empty words, or simply an unreal entity. Maybe it *is* the void, of which brings all things, events, and people to be real. Who knows? A soul could be our mind or our life force of vitality. But what we **do** know is this: *life is what you make of it, so make it sing… make it ring out an echo* – of your own accord.

330. You have love in your heart and thought in

your head. Compose the two together and gather the harmony from thoughtfulness and heart.

331. Let's go. Right now. Let's get this done. *Right now.*

332. Let's get something straight: the world is not for indulging in pleasures or running away from our pains. The world is here for its own order, natural *beyond-human* order, of which we are all part. We live, according to nature, by her rules and her governance, and we seek to grow in what is natural *with* what is natural, not that which is unnatural, impure, foolish, or dull. Therefore, what we should be doing is listening to our nature in that which is natural outside in the world and disregard what is obnoxious, unnatural, or delusional. Disregard pleasure, then, as a hindrance of your true nature, which is the nature of everyone else, which is the nature of the whole world. Pain will heal and mend itself naturally just as our bodies heal after striking wounds. Let it mend, then, and yourself heal; let yourself be natural, and allow yourself to be pure. Allow yourself to

heal in time, and allow yourself to endure. This is the way of letting go, and we must *let it* for us to *go*.

333. Sin only exists in religions, yet there are obvious actions that are bad. Abstain from what is bad, in all your behaviour, thought, and speech and see your life flourish, not flounder. Push through, don't be pulled back. *Name what is bad and stay clear from being pulled back.*

334. If you feel uneasy, know that this is a natural state of a human being. We are subject to emotions, passing, arising and floating away. They are temporary, just as every temporal object of this life. But what is *not* temporary? What is *constant*? What *endures*? – Action. Perseverance. Goodness. Truth, Justice, and Light. Trust, then, in the truth of your action and its goodness, for the rewards will reap in and outside of you – outside to others and your world as our own. Rejoice, then, in the endurance of what is permanent: the world and our very own effects upon our lives.

335. How do you analyze yourself? Do not be witty, do not be passive, do not be lay or

arrogant. You do not know, so why do you claim to? Ignorance falls unto all of us, so why deem yourself as less than human? In so, you are just that very much more of a human, disguising your ignorance as know-how, fabricating what is 'unknown' with what has been shaped as "known". Do away with your ignorance and admit it! Know that you do not know – this is the beginning of wisdom, a wealth of knowledge for you to hold. Now, analyze and see yourself fade away into nothing but what you really are – void and empty of meaning. How do you overcome this? *By looking inside to see.* How do you fill it? – *with your meaning.*

336. What is your aim? – to do good. How do you do this? – by restraining from what's bad. How do you know what is bad? – from experience. What from experience? – from its results. So, what do you do? – aim towards the good. What good will come out of it? – all you will ever need to learn and know.

337. We are called to love our family, enjoy our friends, thrive in kinship and communion with people, but are challenged to not be

attached. What if our family is rotten, if our parents are evil, our brothers and or sisters impure? What is that on you? What you do is yours entirely, and what is theirs is theirs their own. What is not yours in none of your business, nothing to attach to, none of your responsibility or concern. But life, the life of those who truly live, is to be in concord with what is good and just, pure and awakening. So, what to do with family? –Love. Support. Endure. Show generosity, respect, and goodness. Teach them well, then, and be a good member of your family, show your support by being present. Only know that if your well-being is threatened by your family that you must take your steady detachment away from them *on your own*. Be with people who are as true as family instead, and fulfill your own familial role. Show love to those who care and protect your from what is out there, for there is much harmful as much as beautiful out there in our life. Open up to beauty in your relations and see the beauty unfold.

338. Take time away from the things you love

for a couple of reasons: One is to appreciate the love you have for such objects, people, places, and pleasures; another is to refresh your perspective, practicality, and time with those things and people you love. Appreciate and freshen yourself up with what you love.

339. Clear your mind by thinking with focus and direction. Do **not** allow thought to happen *to you* without your own controlled focus. A directed mind will allow only what is permitted by you, by your reason and experience, alone. *Think for yourself.*

340. Remember that you can communicate to yourself to reassure yourself at any time. Your mind can be controlled with thought – this is clear. So, clearly use your own thoughts to move yourself away from doubt, fear, and insecurity. Solidify your experience with your directed thoughts and apply them to your day-to-day life. *Do you worry about your health?* – take note of your feelings at the time you do. *Do you concern yourself with criticisms you receive from family members, friends, or strangers?* – ask yourself whether

it is within your control to let external circumstances and influences affect your will or self-image. *Do you think some writings are too long to read at first glance?* – notice how you got to the end of this read already, and how fast the time has passed. *Communicate with yourself when no one else is around. You will never be lonely again.*

341. Communication and time. One within our power, the other beyond our control. Note how you can influence the one as the other happens naturally **simultaneously**. Focus on the one while letting nature take care of the other – that is, *the nature of time.*

342. Apply yourself to communicate with people to see how vast your knowledge is, to see how vast others' knowledge is to your own. Do not berate yourself on your lack of knowledge or ever put yourself down because you do not know as much as another. We all have our own share of experience and knowledge and time to work on our own share of it in the future. It is only a matter of how you communicate it that forms our knowledge and informs us for the

better. *Never compare what you know to that of others unless it is for discernment.* Comparing yourself or your knowledge with others is a sorry attempt at an unnecessary competitive drive. Rid yourself of this competitive drive. *Just speak, learn and **listen**.*

343. Is there any freedom in memory? If it comes to the happiness someone receives after reminiscing about good experiences with people, about places, or of objects you have loved, then memory serves as a tool for exercising the freedom of their mind. *But do you have to remember everything?* This is impossible – you may remember only what you attend to habitually, naturally in your mind, or what someone reminds you through words and actions. *Does it bring you down when you forget?* If so, remember that memory is only slightly in your control, and slightly, on the other hand, outside of it. So, remember only what you tend to remember: the freedom of thought and its power to help you recall what you want or need. Appointments, destinations, and personal values – remember them well. It only takes a few repetitions of

thinking to memorize what you need to for what must be done. Then *remember*: freedom is found in memory only to a degree. What is that degree? – that is the true freedom found in memory of past happiness to bring it up for the present and for the future.

344. Do you have a favourite pastime, a favourite hobby? Do you make time for it, for them, for *all* of them? How about making time for most of them or only for some? If you are not, *what are you waiting for for them to happen*? The power to schedule your days, availability, and work schedule is at your disposal for your freedom. You do not need to limit your options to only what you believe is attainable, timely, or possible. Better jobs that are suitable to your needs *are* It is only a matter of search and discovery to see who would accommodate to your needs to see what kind of person you want to be in your time. "To be is to do," as Immanuel Kant would say *again*. Accept what is before rearranging your lifestyle and keep in mind what you can do to adjust your time to make it slightly more accommodating. Time is as

precious as you make use of it; so, make use of it and live.

345. Schedule time to think for yourself alone, daily, nightly, or whenever you have a moment to spare. The rewards are peace of mind and a piece of your mind – that is, in serenity.

346. So close, so far: what does it matter? You are here. You are alive. You are reading this right now and you are present at this time. Remember this in time of need – not that you are reading, but – that you are a human being with temporary feelings, subject to passing time, a human who can control their mind with the freedom of your own choice and direction. You decide how to determine your interpretations. You are in control of your thoughts and influences. Let happen what you want to let happen, and let go of what is none of your concern – people's choices, opinions, and characters. Know what is good for you and what is bad for you with discernment through selective good judgment. Allow what is good, avoid what is bad that is in your control. You can

overcome any difficulty with a steady mind and self-control. Make use of these, and use them *now*. Avoid who you would call a bad person or people and see how your life will change for the best.

347. Beauty is found in nature. People are natural beings. But beauty is more than just physical appearance. Beauty is inside of what is natural, is the story behind what is here and there. Beautiful are the trees that stand strong through the force of powerful winds and torturous storms. Beautiful are the words that state the truth that are spoken in front of those who need to hear them. Beautiful are the intentions of good men and women and the actions of the virtuous who act upon them. Beautiful are the virtues that are exemplified by the people who request the best of their use of time. Beauty is, then, an art of what is natural and true, good and virtuous. Look out for what is beautiful and, therefore, share in the beauty of this life – your life that is worth living.

348. Writing is separate from thought – that is pretty clear. Writing is more about

expression than it is that of thinking even about writing. Therefore, not all good things come from well-thought out plans but from expressing yourself through a medium of personal or public use. Write, then, for yourself or for others; the choice is a matter of a 'why', no longer of a 'how'. Why, then? – for composure, for self-assertion, for organizing your thoughts, the reasons for you to write or think to yourself; for change, to inspire, for expressing the truth to be understood are reasons for others to hear or read you. So, have a purpose for writing and write for that purpose; think for that purpose as well.

349. *Know who you are by what you do, say, think, and feel. You also know by what you choose and what you intend. You especially know who you are by what you make happen.* Make things happen for the best; the best is what you now know, so act upon your knowledge and thrive.

350. Pressure creates diamonds. Procrastination is not necessary; your creative energy is necessary. So, create your diamonds with your passion, energy, and internal pressures.

Make use of the suffering you have. Everybody receives their share of suffering. *You are not alone in the creative, painful process.*

351. What to do when you have nothing to do? – *this determines your sense of self and freedom.*

352. High altitudes are reached not only through flight or climbing but through daily practice of the goals you pursue. Meditate and witness your mind transform, your reality transform, your relations change into what is good and true, supportive and caring. Look on high up there… while you keep your feet flat on the ground.

353. Respect your elders, those who are younger than you, and those your age – in a word, *everyone*. Respect should be given to everyone without exception. Even those who wrong you must be treated with goodness if you are to maintain your good will towards all people. Separate a person's ill will and inapt behaviour with who they really are. Then you will see you can respect even those who disrespect you. You can respect their **truer** character without regard to their current actions, words, or character. Respect, but do

not expect to receive any, respect in return. That is the job of self-respect and loving yourself, the fact that no one can pierce through your sense of what is good in you.

354. Disagreements will happen. Nothing is in harmony forever. There is an ebb *and* a flow. Learn to deal, then, with the setbacks and disputes between people with a steady, firm, and resolute mindset. Learn to let go of what you cannot control in an argument: namely, someone's perspective. Accept that not everyone shares the same opinion as you. You can move on and develop your own solid, consistent views. This takes time as the virtue of patience requires of you. So, let go of thinking that all must go smoothly, according to plan. This is *not* how life works out at all times. Life works itself out by you putting in the effort and nature working herself out. So, likewise, *work yourself out*.

355. Fear is within you if allow it to flourish. Courage and goodness and truth are the same. Your will, action, and mindset determine what you spend your time on. Why invest in something like fear when you can

control your superstitions and remove them, when you can use your own good mind with judgment and common sense, with compassion, understanding and without criticism? Construct what is good and truthful, strong and courageous. Deconstruct what makes you fearful by looking at fear straight ahead. You know you have the power to do so. You know you are capable and worthy of fearlessness. *Fearlessness is a word for those who are deserving – for those who have conquered their fear, have felt it, and pushed on. So,* push yourself on.

356. What is the point of looking back when you could look straight ahead? What is the point of checking how you appear when you can act, think, speak, and choose in all three? Why do you hurt yourself by thinking you are better than someone other than yourself? We are equal – action is the proof. We start at a baseline and develop from the past into right here and now. Don't fool yourself into delusions – know exactly what life is about and move on to make it the best as it can possibly be. Life is about setting goals

and setting out to do them. States of affairs become easy once you know they are possible. All you must do is work and continue. So, *con-tin-ue*. Life is to do, then be.

357. Why speak mumbo jumbo when you can speak easily, honestly and for real? Concern yourself with truth and not how others will take your constructive criticisms. You do not need anyone to support your truth to make it more true... you have already validated it with your thoughts and actions. Nothing is more powerful than these – your sound mind and action.

358. This day and age we rely on much to get by. Try for a day to be *without* objects of "necessity", what you desire and crave that you "love more than anything else", that you "cannot live without." Check and see if you will survive – without your phone, your computer, your attachments.

359. Persistence means to continue when you want to quit, when you wanted to quit five minutes ago, ten, or twenty. One way to push through is to set up time limits for your work, just as breaks are scheduled at

your job according to a plan. Is it 7:31 pm? Work until 8 pm. Have you passed by 8 pm since you have been working? Work until 8:30 pm. Push yourself to the limits you never would have thought you could have achieved through time management and a will to set yourself out to do more. *Do more than you imagined.*

360. Luck is a fickle friend, if a friend at all. If it were a true friend, it would not let you down or cause any disappointment. Therefore, luck is no friend at all. It is subject to chance and fluctuation, nothing that a true friend would admire or take on as a real friend. So, don't rely on luck to serve you or any of any one of your needs. It is **work** that you must rely on that must be taken up to improve what it is you call **luck**. Luck is merely your actions turning back towards you, either for the better, or for the worse. Make your actions great and reap in the results from all you do. *In the game of luck, action is the victor.* And so, you act outside of luck's grasp.

361. Determine what? – your actions, behaviour,

your studies, and the truth from you and yourself alone. Set out to do what? – to pursue your ambitions, dreams, long-term goals, what you set out to do. What are you here for? – for whatever you know you want or need to be. What do you want to do with your life? – to be a good person and serve others in that process. Love the life that you lead – *I cannot say it enough, for it is what you need.*

362. Should you push yourself to do what you don't want to, or risk failing if you do? Well, I didn't want to write right now. I didn't want to continue writing until right now. What if I had never pushed myself, then? *What if I never started from the beginning?* I would not be at three hundred sixty one out of how many?

363. Where do our likes come from? – the past and present, guided by the present, future, or past. Where do we get to grow up? – in no choice of our own until we mature. So, what do we do from where we are? – we set ourselves out to pursue our future without having its pressure hold us down, to

live where we want to live – either home or away – and to do what we know is good, deserving, and true. What are these three attributes? – the way out of misery, sadness, and suffering. The right way is the only way, and the wrong way is every other. *Know what's right from what's wrong*: these are our likes and dislikes, respectively.

364. Do you know how far you have come? From an infant, you have grown into a toddler, to a child, to a teen and now (possibly) an adult. You may grow further, but you have already made it through puberty, bullying, teasing, opposition, stress, and pains. You combat these through stresses up to this day and find new ways to cope and move on. You have suffered through anxieties and worry, depression and overeating, undereating, pleasure-seeking and freedom-chasing. You have swept past all these things and what is left to remain? – you and your developed mind. How about all you have accomplished? Have you done right things, wrong, or things worth nothing at all? Remember the setbacks that you have conquered and

the victories you have won. The losers are the concepts fallen from your mind and the fallen are those ideas that held you back from the beginning. Make no use of such past mistakes and live your life rightly, justly and true. You know you have moved on and it was because of you and the people you knew that pushed you through. Thank them and continue to be you, be true, and do you.

365. What you add to your mind is what you will see in time. What you subtract from your mind is what you no longer have control over.

366. Love is a delicate thing, a torturous thing, yet a beautiful thing. You must give yourself up for another, and trust that another will keep you afloat happily with serenity in peace and freedom. Attachment is what you two shy away from although you spend much of your time together. An interdependent sort of love is the best kind of love where two lovers could flourish to be themselves and even more so with each other. Connection is the necessity. Communication is

the key. The lock is openness and the door is to understand. To understand is to love unconditionally and to give completely to the way you receive yourself – from yourself and from your other. Love yourself; love one another.

367. How do you know that you are on the right track? When you smile at others and others smile back. When you give yourself freely and receive tenfold back. As you let go of bad people and welcome good company, as you let go of worries and allow thinking to replace them, your life becomes righteous and worthy, direct and clear. A purpose of your life is to give, right here, now, so you can give and receive, love and be free. Happiness, if not on its way, is surely, after all that, right and truly here. You know you're on track when you're happy right here despite what you want in the future or what you've wanted from the past. Happiness is the track, and you will come to know it lasts.

368. Spirituality is the connection of another being and yourself, the source of this world and your creative energy. Connections with

others are potential for understanding, compassion, mutual interest, and mutual satisfaction, which is love and spiritual living. New age spirituality does not need to be the way. What shows more are the ancients who have paved our way. If you dare to seek the truth and understand what ancients say, you will find the wisdom and the truth to surely be on your way.

369. Thinking has its time, but so does laying back and relaxing your mind. Energy has its time to shine in creative endeavours, in release, in work, at play, and in thought, but also in its time to lie down, breathe in, and let go. Feelings have their time to be understood but a healthy distance from them is crucial for separating yourself from the inner world inside you. Everything, then, has its own time, place, and special circumstance – *from a former teacher of mine.*

370. Direct your thoughts and see your life change in front of your mind: *in front of eyes of your very own.*

371. Turn around to remember what has been behind you, but do not ever change your

course on forwards. Once your course is set, once you are sure of it, continue to move straight on ahead. You can check behind you, but should never turn back. Be resolute in your decisions and keep moving ahead; commitment is the only way to stay consistent in what you do and think, say and choose. *Do it consistently, and be, rightly so, far long ahead.*

372. Your time here is all you will ever have, *that* along with your actions. Intentions mean nothing without action, words, thoughts, or decisions that correspond to their truth. This is harsh but true: true words were never supposed to sound pleasant to the ear.

373. With your time here, understand what you must do to make yourself and those around you love, grow in understanding – understanding what you need to do and take into consideration. What's the next step? – do, *do*, **do**. Only lay back and relax as the day comes to an end. *Act and you shall receive.*

374. *Everything will go away* – this is the nature of our world. Has a new person come into your life? – they will surely go away one day.

Do you have a family or dear friends? – they, also, will move away and be gone one day. Is this emotionally disturbing? – question why that is so. Change is the nature of our world and our existence. We must, therefore, grow and detach from all emotions to things impermanent and temporary, things that do not last forever. **Knowledge** frees us from becoming subject to another or tied down to an emotion, a person, situation, pass of time. Knowledge will move us to appreciate the people who are here for us now and teach us how to act among them or those we love with respect and an enduring love *while they are still here*. The moments that matter are the ones where we are still here – in mind and in the present. *Accept what's natural. Know you must change someday as well.*

375. Teach whenever you can teach, as truthfully as you can teach, to those around you, older, younger, or the same age. Your influence may change their mind or their world ...or simply nothing at all.

376. Make a solid and honest pledge right here and now: *Only*, and I mean ***only***, focus on

what you tell yourself to do without any distraction of checking what others think you're doing. The behaviours of others are for the study of appearances, as that is all they really are. Focus, then, and strive to make yourself as immune to appearances as possible; at once, however, consider that you are just an appearance to others, too.

377. You have made it. You have done what you have set out to do. Now do you understand how this world works? You put in the effort, and happiness shines its face forward through your actions, *through you*. Thank yourself for what you have accomplished. You've done it, so now is time to celebrate. So,***CELEBRATE!***

378. A final word of advice: *Do what makes you happy, what you are good at, what you can excel in. You will never regret it when you have it to hold for a while.*

379. You have *everything* to gain in consistency and the practice of time, so **make** the minutes count in each second you put forward.

380. The best is yet to come, but better can come at any time... even *now*.

381. Take these passages with you, wherever you may be, as I take these, my own, with me.
382. You are done. You can rest now.
383. Note to self: keep going.

www.ingramcontent.com/pod-product-compliance
Lightning Source LLC
Chambersburg PA
CBHW070045120526
44589CB00035B/2317